VINCE LOMBARDI ON LEADERSHIP

VINCE LOMBARDI ON LEADERSHIP

Life Lessons from a Five-Time
NFL Championship Coach

PAT WILLIAMS

with JIM DENNEY

Advantage®

Published by Advantage, Charleston, South Carolina.
Member of Advantage Media Group.

ADVANTAGE is a registered trademark and the Advantage colophon is a trademark of Advantage Media Group, Inc.

Printed in the United States of America.
Cover photos courtesy of *Green Bay Press-Gazette* archives.

ISBN: 978-1-59932-518-7
LCCN: 2015945002

This publication is designed to provide accurate and authoritative information in regard to the subject matter covered. It is sold with the understanding that the publisher is not engaged in rendering legal, accounting, or other professional services. If legal advice or other expert assistance is required, the services of a competent professional person should be sought.

Advantage Media Group is proud to be a part of the Tree Neutral® program. Tree Neutral offsets the number of trees consumed in the production and printing of this book by taking proactive steps such as planting trees in direct proportion to the number of trees used to print books. To learn more about Tree Neutral, please visit **www.treeneutral.com**. To learn more about Advantage's commitment to being a responsible steward of the environment, please visit **www.advantagefamily.com/green**

Advantage Media Group is a publisher of business, self-improvement, and professional development books and online learning. We help entrepreneurs, business leaders, and professionals share their Stories, Passion, and Knowledge to help others Learn & Grow. Do you have a manuscript or book idea that you would like us to consider for publishing? Please visit **advantagefamily.com** or call **1.866.775.1696**.

Dedicated
to Royce Boyles, Green Bay Packers historian,
who went way out of his way to help me
track down Lombardi's former players and staff.
This book never could have happened without
Royce's invaluable insight and help.

CONTENTS

ACKNOWLEDGMENTS

With deep appreciation I acknowledge the support and guidance of the following people who helped make this book possible:

Special thanks to Alex Martins, Dan DeVos, and Rich DeVos of the Orlando Magic.

And a special salute to Mark Murphy, president of the Green Bay Packers.

Hats off to my associate Andrew Herdliska; my proofreader, Ken Hussar; and my ace typist, Fran Thomas.

Thanks also to my writing partner, Jim Denney, for his superb contributions in shaping this manuscript.

Hearty thanks also go to Adam Witty, founder and president of Advantage Media Group, and the entire Advantage publishing team for their able assistance in making this book a reality.

And, finally, special thanks and appreciation go to my wife, Ruth, and to my wonderful and supportive family. They are truly the backbone of my life.

INTRODUCTION

THE SEVEN SIDES
OF VINCE LOMBARDI

*Leaders are made; they are not born. They are made
by hard effort, which is the price all of us must pay
to achieve any goal that is worthwhile.*[1]
—Vince Lombardi

I once had a conversation with Forrest Gregg on my local sports talk radio show in Orlando. He was an offensive tackle for the Green Bay Packers from 1956 to 1970, so he was in Green Bay during both the pre-Lombardi "wilderness years" and the "golden age" of the Lombardi Era. Gregg suffered through the infamous 1958 season, when the team finished 1-10-1—the worst record in Packers history. And he vividly recalled the day in 1959 when Vince Lombardi conducted his first practice as Packers head coach.

"Coach Lombardi was working with the quarterbacks and receivers," Gregg told me. "No one on the team knew what to expect from our new coach. He was a rookie head coach, and most of us had never even heard of him before.

"We had this one receiver who had great speed, great hands, but he would slack off in practice. He always got away with it under previous coaches—they never said a word to him, no matter how much he goofed off in practice. Well, Coach Lombardi sent this guy out on a route, but he didn't run the pattern the way Lombardi told him to. He was about twenty yards downfield when Coach Lombardi started yelling at him. Lombardi was still yelling when the guy got back to the huddle.

"Coach Lombardi had announced, loud and clear, that the Packers were under new management. That moment on the first day of practice told me we finally had a *leader* in charge of the Packers. From then on, I was sold on Vince Lombardi."

Vince Lombardi was indeed a leader. Though his entire career as an NFL head coach only lasted ten seasons, he never had a losing season. He coached the Packers from the absolute cellar of the NFL to a winning season in 1959, the NFL championship game in the 1960 season, then to NFL world championships in 1961, 1962, 1965, 1966, and 1967 (including Super Bowls I and II). In his ten seasons as an NFL head coach, Lombardi compiled a career record of 105-35-6.

In July 2009, *The Sporting News* ranked the fifty greatest coaches of all time, in all sports, as selected by a blue ribbon panel of sports writers and coaches. Number two on that list, second only to UCLA basketball coach John Wooden, was Vince Lombardi. In other words, Vince Lombardi was selected as the *greatest football coach of all time*. If he had not died of cancer at age 57, in the prime of his career, there's no telling what he might have achieved.

I have been studying leadership throughout my adult life, and of all the leaders I've studied, Vince Lombardi is about as close to a complete leader as it's possible to be. He was not a perfect human being, but he understood leadership, and he knew how to achieve results through people. The results speak for themselves.

I have researched this book by tracking down and interviewing the people who played for Coach Lombardi—not only in Green Bay but also at Fordham University, West Point, and the Washington Redskins. I've gathered stories and insights from Bart Starr, Paul Hornung, Gary Knafelc, Willie Davis, Jerry Kramer, Sonny Jurgensen, Boyd Dowler, Zeke Bratkowski, and many more. I have even interviewed opposing players, coaches, officials, and secretaries who knew him. As a result, you'll find fresh new leadership insights in this book that have never been published before.

In my study of leadership, I've identified seven essential ingredients or dimensions that form the essence of leadership. I call these ingredients "The Seven Sides of Leadership." A leader who has all seven of these qualities is well equipped for leadership. The good news for you and me as leaders is that these characteristics are all learnable skills. Though most of us are naturally gifted in at least a few of these skills, we can learn, grow, and improve our mastery of any leadership skills we lack.

Vince Lombardi was the quintessential role model of all of the Seven Sides of Leadership—but he wasn't naturally gifted in all of them. As we will see, Lombardi himself was a student of leadership. When he was a young man, he didn't exhibit any traits to suggest he would one day become the greatest football coach of all time. The leadership skills he studied and acquired are available to you and me. Here are "The Seven Sides of Leadership," which Coach Vince Lombardi so richly exemplified:

1. Vision. Great leaders have the ability to envision what the future should look like and the ability to chart a course for getting there. Visionary leadership is not the ability to foresee the future but to invent the future, to shape the future, and to influence the team or organization in such a way as to turn the leader's vision into reality.

2. Communication Skills. The ability to communicate persuasively and effectively is an essential tool of leadership. Once a leader has envisioned the future, he or she must be able to communicate that vision to the troops. Leaders influence their followers by communicating their vision, their values, and their enthusiasm, especially through public speaking.

3. People Skills. Great leaders know what excites and motivates people. They know how to encourage and empower their followers to work together toward a common goal. People skills are vital tools for influencing others—and people skills can be learned and improved with practice.

4. Character. Leadership is influence, so a leader must be an influential role model. The people you lead take their cue from you. They choose whether or not to trust you and buy into your agenda—and they base their trust on their perception of your character. Good character is essential to your leadership influence.

5. Competence. Followers want to know that their leader has the competence and competitiveness to lead them to victory. Great leaders have a track record of competence and success. They demonstrate an unquenchable will to win and an unrelenting competitive spirit.

6. Boldness. Great leaders are decisive, courageous, and willing to take bold action. Great leaders never seem outwardly uncertain or indecisive but display complete confidence, especially in times of adversity. Confidence is contagious and can be a force multiplier when the chips are down.

7. A Serving Heart. A leader without a serving heart is just a boss. Great leaders make policies, enforce rules, hold subordinates accountable, and command respect—yet great leaders are also servants of the people they lead. A leader must make sure that people are properly trained, equipped, motivated, and empowered. It's the leader's job, as the servant of the troops, to make sure they have everything they need to succeed.

The book you hold in your hands is the fourth in a series of books I've written about great coaches and their legacy of leadership. The first three are *Bear Bryant on Leadership* (written with Tommy Ford), *Bobby Bowden on Leadership* (written with Rob Wilson), and *Tom Osborne on Leadership* (written with Mike Babcock). My goal in all of these books is to peer behind the legend and take the true measure of each leader according to this seven-sided yardstick.

As we're about to see, Coach Vince Lombardi had all seven of those qualities. The Seven Sides of Leadership will serve you well in any leadership role, in any field of endeavor—in the sports, business, government, military, academic, or religious leadership worlds. I certainly don't claim that I have been able to plumb the depths of this man's leadership life, but I do believe we've come as close as anyone can get to uncovering Lombardi's leadership secrets. If you want to improve your winning percentage as a leader, then one of the most instructive lives you can study is Coach Vince Lombardi.

I'd like you to meet Vince Lombardi.

Pat Williams
Orlando, Florida
August 15, 2015

CHAPTER 1

THE VISIONARY LEADERSHIP OF VINCE LOMBARDI

The best coaches know what the end result looks like, whether it's an offensive play, a defensive play, a defensive coverage, or just some idea of the organization. If you don't know what the end result is supposed to look like, you can't get there.[2]
—Vince Lombardi

Vince Lombardi was born in 1913 in the Sheepshead Bay section of Brooklyn to Enrico "Harry" Lombardi, a meat cutter, and Matilda "Mattie" Izzo Lombardi. Both the Lombardi and Izzo clans lived in Sheepshead Bay, so Vince grew up in a working-class neighborhood, surrounded by family. Young Vince's life revolved around the Catholic Church. He was an altar boy at St. Mark's, and from his earliest years until his hospitalization before his death, Vince attended Mass every day.

Italian Americans suffered hostility and discrimination in those days, and the insults young Vince endured gave him a great empathy for people who were marginalized and mistreated. At age 15, he graduated from the eighth grade and began a six-year program for the priesthood at Brooklyn's Cathedral College of the Immaculate Conception, playing off-campus football in his spare time. After four years at Cathedral College, he abandoned his plan to be a priest. Enrolling at St. Francis Prep in Fresh Meadows, Queens, he played fullback for the Prep Terriers.

Lombardi attended Fordham University on a football scholarship. Though undersized at five feet eight inches and 172 pounds, Lombardi demonstrated speed and aggressiveness on the field. In 1936, his senior year, he played right guard as one of the "Seven Blocks of Granite," Fordham's offensive line.

Early in a game against the University of Pittsburgh, Lombardi lined up against Tony Matisi, a 215-pound All-American. This was the leather helmet era—no face guards. At the snap, Matisi leaped out of his stance and drove his elbow into Lombardi's mouth. Teeth and blood went flying, and Lombardi's mouth was deeply gashed. He stayed in the game, playing most of the game with blood constantly pooling in his mouth. After the game, the team doctor used 30 stitches to sew up his mouth. To get through it, Lombardi mentally repeated the words his father taught him: "Hurt is in the mind."[3]

Lombardi's fabled toughness as a coach may be traceable to that smash in the mouth. Lombardi could honestly tell his players he demanded nothing of them that he hadn't summoned from within himself as a player. He expected his players to play hurt and walk off the pain—unless there was a risk of doing injury to themselves.

That year, Fordham went undefeated until the final game of the season against New York University. NYU was supposed to be a pushover—but somebody forgot to tell NYU. The NYU Violets upended the Fordham Rams 7-6, scuttling Fordham's plans to play in the Rose Bowl.[4] It was a bitter loss for Vince Lombardi—and a lesson he never forgot. As a coach, he would always push his teams twice as hard before a game against a so-called "pushover" team. He learned never to take any opponent for granted—especially the supposedly "easy" ones.

NO SUBSTITUTE FOR VICTORY

Lombardi graduated from Fordham in 1937, during the depths of the Depression. He had no vision for his future, so he tried semi-pro-football and debt collecting—and discovered that he was under-sized for football and too big-hearted for debt collection. Encouraged by his father to try a career in law, he enrolled in Fordham's law school. After one semester, he decided he wasn't meant to be a lawyer, either.

In 1939, Vince Lombardi's life turned a corner when one of his old Fordham teammates, Andy Palau, was hired as the football coach at St. Cecilia, a tiny Catholic high school in Englewood, New Jersey. The entire co-ed student body numbered fewer than 400. Palau hired Lombardi as an assistant coach and a teacher of chemistry, physics, biology, and Latin. Lombardi was surprised to find that he liked coaching and teaching—which, to him, were the same thing. He taught at St. Cecilia for eight years, three years as an assistant, and five years as head coach. It was Lombardi's only head coaching job until he was hired to coach the Green Bay Packers.

Saint Cecilia's athletic director, Father Tim Moore, paid Lombardi a little extra to coach varsity basketball as well. Lombardi later joked, "Father Moore took a vow of poverty, then lived up to it with me." Lombardi shared office space with Father Tim, who became Lombardi's spiritual advisor, mentor, confessor, and eventually an unofficial assistant coach. Lombardi could go to Father Tim anytime, anyplace, to make his confession. Neither man felt the need of confession booth. Lombardi and Father Tim remained close friends until Lombardi's death.

In 1940, Lombardi married Marie Planitz over her father's objections. A Wall Street stockbroker, Mr. Planitz didn't want his daughter marrying an Italian. Biographer Chris Havel observed: "The life of a coach's wife had its drawbacks, as Marie knew quite well, saying, 'I wasn't married to him more than one week when I said to myself, *Marie Planitz, you've made the greatest mistake of your life.*'"[5] Vince and Marie had two children, son Vince Jr., born in 1942, and daughter Susan, born in 1947.

In 1947 and 1948, Lombardi coached football and basketball at Fordham. After the 1948 football season, he took an assistant coaching position at the US Military Academy at West Point. This would prove to be another key turning point in his leadership career. At West Point, Lombardi was offensive line coach and an understudy to famed Army head coach Colonel Earl "Red" Blaik. Under Blaik's mentorship, Lombardi developed a unique coaching style that was all his own, though heavily influenced by the strict Army discipline of West Point. Lombardi's coaching was also infused with the stern, demanding spirituality he had learned from the Jesuits at Fordham.

Red Blaik's influence on Lombardi was immense. Coach Blaik was an innovator who pioneered the two-platoon system (utilizing separate offensive and defensive units) that eventually became the standard of the game. It was Blaik, drawing on his Army background, who coined the football term "platoon." So Vince Lombardi was strategically positioned on the cutting edge of football innovation.

While at West Point, Lombardi had the privilege of getting to know one of his all-time heroes, General Douglas MacArthur.

After every Army game, Lombardi delivered the game film to a film processing facility on Long Island. He would return with cans of processed game film, and, at the direction of Coach Blaik, he would stop at General MacArthur's spacious penthouse apartment atop the Waldorf-Astoria Towers in midtown Manhattan. There, Lombardi would screen the film for the legendary general.

Typically, MacArthur would wear a gray flannel bathrobe with his varsity letter sewed on, and he would pepper Lombardi with questions as the film rolled. MacArthur's knowledge of the game was encyclopedic, and he knew every Army player's jersey number, position, and stats.

Lombardi felt awed and honored to personally know one of his heroes. He often quoted insights from General MacArthur in speeches to his players or to business groups. Lombardi said of MacArthur, "I can vividly remember him saying that 'competitive sports keeps alive in us a spirit and vitality. It teaches the strong to know when they are weak and the brave to face themselves when they are afraid. To be proud and unbowed in defeat and yet humble and gentle in victory. And to master ourselves before we attempt to master others. And to learn to laugh, yet never forget how to weep. And to give the predominance of courage over timidity.'"[6]

Vince Lombardi's competitiveness may have been an inborn trait, but that trait was confirmed and formalized into memorable axioms under the influence of his two role models from his West Point days, Coach Blaik and General MacArthur. It was Red Blaik who drilled into Lombardi, "The purpose of the game is to win. To dilute the will to win is to destroy the purpose of the game." And it was General MacArthur who famously said, "There is no substitute for victory."[7]

THE MAN WHO SAVED THE PACKERS

In 1954, after five seasons at West Point, 41-year-old Vince Lombardi moved to the NFL, joining the coaching staff of Jim Lee Howell, the new head coach of the New York Giants. At that time, the game of football was becoming more complex and specialized, and Howell was an early adopter of new ideas, including Red Blaik's platoon system. So it was only natural for Howell to recruit Blaik's assistant, Vince Lombardi, to help him implement two-platoon football.

Howell crafted an executive role for himself, delegating authority and responsibility to two top assistants (today, the titles for those positions would be offensive coordinator and defensive coordinator). Howell's offensive assistant was Vince Lombardi, and his defensive assistant was Tom Landry, who would later have a Hall of Fame career as head coach of the Dallas Cowboys. In addition to coaching, Landry was on the field as a defensive back and punter. As Lombardi's biographer David Maraniss noted, "Howell readily acknowledged the talents of Lombardi and Landry and joked self-deprecatingly that his main function was to make sure the footballs had air in them."[8]

Under prior coach Steve Owen, the Giants had finished the 1953 season with a dismal 3-9 record. The coaching triumvirate of Howell, Lombardi, and Landry led the Giants to winning seasons in 1954 and 1955, followed by an NFL championship in 1956, defeating George Halas's Chicago Bears 47-7.

Lombardi wasn't happy as an assistant coach. Having endured prejudice all his life, he believed anti-Italian attitudes were preventing him from landing a head-coaching job, especially in the South. After applying unsuccessfully for numerous college positions, Lombardi told Giants owner Wellington Mara, "Here I am, an Italian, forty-two years old, and nobody wants me. Nobody will take me."[9] Though Lombardi despaired of ever attaining his goal of a head coaching job, he continued to plan, dream, and envision what he would do if he ever got the chance.

What Lombardi didn't realize was that the stars were already beginning to align for him over the frozen tundra of Green Bay, Wisconsin. By the end of 1957, the Packers had gone through three coaches in ten years, compiling a record of 36-83-1. In 1958, when no one thought it could get any worse, it got worse. The Packers promoted backfield coach Ray "Scooter" McLean to head coach, and he coached the Packers to a worst-ever record of 1-10-1. Sportswriter Red Smith summed up the season this way: "The Packers underwhelmed ten opponents, overwhelmed one, and whelmed one."[10]

Was the team that bad? No. In fact, there were six future Hall of Famers on the team during the Season of Shame. The problem wasn't a lack of talent. The problem was leadership. Scooter McLean didn't understand how leadership works. He wanted to be liked, to be one of the guys. He'd often play poker with his players during training camp and on the road—and he'd end up owing them money. He thought he was buddying up to them, but he was actually losing their respect.

Vince Lombardi understood the correct balance between loving your players and wanting to buddy up to them. He once said that a leader should never try to "close the gap" between himself and his team. He should love his team, serve his team, and sacrifice for his team—but he should never try to be one of the guys. "If he does," Lombardi concluded, "he is no longer what he must be. He must walk a tightrope between the consent he must win and the control he must exert."[11]

Coach McLean was never able to walk that tightrope. His players ignored team meetings, flouted the dress code, and slacked off during practice—yet McLean could never get tough with them. He had no plan for motivating his players, no strategic vision for winning games, and (according to quarterback Bart Starr) he had no idea what plays to call or what players to use for any given situation. Packers receiver Gary Knafelc recalled that Coach McLean "was a great guy but he had no leadership qualities. He was not demanding."[12]

The Green Bay Packers are unique as an NFL franchise in that the team doesn't have one wealthy owner or an ownership group like other teams. It's a nonprofit corporation owned by the Green Bay community. The fans themselves are the shareholders. The Packers have a great tradition dating back to its founding by player–coach Curly Lambeau in 1919. During the Lambeau era, the Packers won six national championships (1929, 1930, 1931, 1936, 1939, and 1944). But by the time Scooter McLean took over as head coach in 1958, the Packers had already been in decline for more than a decade.

During those years of humiliation, Green Bay earned a new nickname: "Siberia." College football players had nightmares of being drafted by the Packers. Coaches of other NFL teams maintained discipline by threatening to trade players to Green Bay. Attendance at Packers games steadily declined. Finally, during the 1958 season, Coach McLean led the team into a black hole of despair. Not only were the Packers fans and shareholders furious, but other NFL owners also talked of booting the Packers out of the league. The very existence of the Packers franchise was in jeopardy.

The Packers executive committee scouted the coaching landscape in search of someone to save the storied franchise from extinction. One name came to the top: Forest "Evy" Evashevski, head football coach at the University of Iowa. His 1958 Hawkeyes had compiled an 8–1–1 record, winning the Big Ten Conference, and besting the California Golden Bears in the 1959 Rose Bowl.

The second name on the list was an assistant coach at the New York Giants, somebody named Lombardi. His last head-coaching job had been at a high school in New Jersey in the 1940s. There was little enthusiasm for this Lombardi fellow. The committee pinned its hopes on Evashevski.

Coach Evashevski made a secret four-hour visit to Green Bay, meeting with the Packers executive committee and touring the facility. At the end of the visit, Evashevski's mind was made up. He told the committee he would remain in Iowa.

Vince Lombardi was in the kitchen of his Fair Haven, New Jersey, home when the phone rang. Packers personnel manager Jack Vainisi introduced himself and said, "I'm curious to know whether you're interested in coaching the Green Bay Packers." Yes, Lombardi said, he was very interested.

Lombardi flew to Green Bay for his tour and interview. He met the executive directors in a conference room at the H. C. Prange Department Store, and he did far more listening than talking. When questioned about his background, Lombardi mentioned that he had been trained by Jesuits at Fordham, whereupon one of the Green Bay directors brightened and said, "I was trained by the Jesuits at Marquette," and another said, "And I was taught by the Jesuits at Gonzaga!" At that moment, Lombardi knew he was among friends.

When the directors asked Lombardi about his ideas for restoring the Packers to their former glory, he was ready. He had studied the roster, and he knew there was plenty of winning talent to work with. He described the changes he had made in coordinating the offense of the New York Giants, and how he expected similar approaches to work in Green Bay. He would have a better idea of what he could achieve in Green Bay after he looked at game film, but he was confident that he could take the Packers back to the top of the league where they belonged. Said one member of the Packers executive committee, "He grabbed our attention from the first minute. He knew where he was going. In football terminology, he knew his game plan."[13]

In short, Vince Lombardi was a leader with a vision.

The most attractive part of the job to Lombardi was that he would have enormous authority and autonomy to shape the destiny of the Packers—and to shape his own destiny. He would be hired not only as head coach but also as general manager of the Green Bay Packers, which would give him power over personnel decisions. "That's the only way I'd take the job," Lombardi said at the time. "I doubt if I would have come just as coach. This is a better challenge, a better opportunity."[14] Lombardi officially took over on February 2, 1959. When reporters asked if he really believed he could turn the Green Bay Packers into winners, Lombardi replied, "I have never been associated with a loser, and I don't expect to be now."[15]

The team quickly learned there was a new sheriff in town. Coach Lombardi didn't care if his players liked him. He wasn't interested in being their buddies. He demanded their respect—and he earned it. The new training and practice regimen was strict and physically punishing—and it paid off during the 1959 football season. In game after game, Lombardi's Packers proved themselves to be better trained and better conditioned than their opponents. The 1959 Packers finished with a record of 7-5, and Vince Lombardi was named Coach of the Year in an AP poll of sports journalists.

The fans in Green Bay were ecstatic. In 1960, the Packers improved to 8-4, and every home game was a sellout (in fact, Lambeau Field has been sold out, season after season, ever since). The Packers capped off the 1960 season with a trip to the NFL Championship Game against the Philadelphia Eagles—a thriller of a game that I attended with my dad. The game ended when a Packers comeback attempt failed ten yards short of the goal line. The heartbreaking final score: Eagles 17, Packers 13.

Coach Lombardi blamed himself for the loss, having passed up two easy field goal opportunities and going for it on fourth down. Both attempts failed. Those six points would have won the game. Lombardi promised his players, "This will never happen again. You will never lose another championship."[16]

He kept that vow.

Lombardi coached the Packers to victory in their next nine post-season games. In 1961, the Packers capped an 11-3 season by shutting out Lombardi's old team, the New York Giants, 37-0 in the NFL championship game. It was the team's first title since 1944. Lombardi coached the Packers to a total of five NFL championships, including Super Bowls I and II. Lombardi not only saved the Packers from extinction, but he also brought the title back to Title Town.

He stepped down as Packers head coach after the 1967 NFL season, staying on as the team's general manager through the 1968 season. In 1969, Lombardi returned to coaching, becoming head coach and general manager of the Washington Redskins. He coached the Redskins to a record of 7–5–2, the team's first winning record in 14 years.

In the summer of 1970, as Lombardi was preparing to coach his second season with the Redskins, he was admitted to Georgetown University Hospital for tests related to digestive tract problems he had been suffering from—and trying to ignore—for more than two years. The tests revealed he had an advanced, aggressive, fast-growing form of colon cancer. On September 3, 1970, the cancer claimed Vince Lombardi's life.

INSTILLING THE VISION

With that overview of Vince Lombardi's life and career in mind, let's take a closer look at Lombardi's career with the Packers. After accepting the position in Green Bay, the first thing Lombardi did was go to church and pray. He knew he was going to need strength from beyond himself to meet this challenge.

The next thing he did was set up a movie projector in his basement and watch hundreds of reels of game film. He ran the 16mm projector backward and forward, studying each individual player. He charted plays on yellow legal pads, designing some plays around the abilities of specific players. He made decisions about which players to keep—and which to cut. He knew he had strong talent on offense—talent that would become even stronger under his coaching. But it quickly became clear that the Packers defense was a problem that could only be fixed with trades and personnel changes.[17]

Lombardi made some interesting choices in rebuilding the Packers coaching staff. For example, he hired Norb Hecker as defensive backfield coach—a man without coaching experience, just eight years of playing experience in the NFL. Hecker's former coaches told Lombardi he knew the game and had good character—and that was good enough for Lombardi.

Lombardi hired veteran 49ers coach, Phil Bengtson, as defensive coordinator, John "Red" Cochran as offensive backfield coach, Tom Fears as receivers coach, and Bill Austin as offensive line coach. Lombardi's staff was an eclectic mix of young and old, rookies and veterans. The sole common denominator: each man had a reputation for intense commitment and good character.

With his coaching staff in place, Lombardi began trading and drafting talent. He acquired Henry Jordan and Bill Quinlan from the Cleveland Browns and teamed them with Packers veteran Dave "Hawg" Hanner; he would acquire Willie Davis from the Browns the following year, creating one of the most dominant defensive lines in the NFL. He brought in veteran defensive back Emlen Tunnell from the New York Giants—a decision that Royce Boyles, co-author of *The Lombardi Legacy*, described to me as "very close to the greatest personnel move that Lombardi ever made." Tunnell was the consummate professional, and he brought maturity and discipline to the Packers defense. And because he had such stature and respect among the players, Royce said, Tunnell "made it okay to come and play in Siberia. Lombardi was the coach on the field—but Emlen Tunnell became Lombardi's coach in the locker room. He was viewed as royalty by the other players, and his mature presence helped to maintain discipline throughout the team."

To reinforce his offense, Lombardi brought in players like guard Fred "Fuzzy" Thurston from Baltimore, running back Lew Carpenter from Cleveland, and quarterback Lamar McHan from the St. Louis Cardinals. Lombardi initially selected McHan as his starting quarterback, but an injury early in the season sent McHan to the sidelines. McHan's replacement, Bart Starr, would go on to have a Hall of Fame career.

Lombardi envisioned the running game as the centerpiece of the new Packers offense. The focus of the running game would be versatile running back Paul Hornung, who could not only pound the ball but also pass, receive, and kick. Hornung was a hard-working, self-sacrificing Heisman-winner who intensely wanted to win. Lombardi saw his own competitive spirit reflected in Hornung's eyes, and he envisioned Hornung as the emotional spark plug of the team.

"Lombardi had the eye of a jeweler for talent," Royce Boyles told me. "He could spot talent and envision that talent in new roles, and remake it to suit his vision. When Willie Davis played for the Cleveland Browns, he was an offensive lineman. Lombardi brought him to Green Bay and made a Hall of Fame defensive end out of him. Herb Adderley had been an outstanding running back at Michigan State, but he never played a down from scrimmage as a Packers running back in the regular season—Lombardi remade him as a Hall of Fame cornerback. And Lombardi turned USC quarterback Willie Wood into a Hall of Fame safety for Green Bay.

"It's interesting that Lombardi, who came from a background as an offensive coach, performed much of this alchemy by moving a guy from offense to defense. That's an amazing gift—the ability to look at a player and envision an entirely different future for him and to be right every time."

Lombardi had a clear vision for what the Green Bay Packers could become under his leadership—and he assembled his team in accordance with that vision. Then, he began to instill that vision into his coaching staff and players. To give his players the vision of themselves as elite professionals, he instituted a dress code: gray shirt and tie, plus a Packers-green sports coat. On the first day of practice, Lombardi addressed the team, telling them, "You were chosen to be a Green Bay Packer."

Whenever Lombardi saw his players delivering a second-rate effort, he would use that vision of their potential greatness to motivate them to work harder. For example, in one early practice, Lombardi was running his players through his infamous "nutcracker" drill, when he noticed that linebacker Ray Nitschke was dogging it.

"Mr. Nitschke," Lombardi called out, "I have read that you are the best linebacker in the NFL. But after watching you just then, I find it hard to believe. Now, do it again!"

On the next whistle, Nitschke exploded forward, grabbed a rookie lineman by his shoulder pads, lifted the unfortunate man off his feet, tossed him into running back Jim Taylor, and kept going.[18] Paul Hornung recalled, "It took them two minutes to get the rookie to come to."[19]

That was exactly what Lombardi wanted to see. The moment Lombardi gave Ray Nitschke a vision of himself as "the best linebacker in the NFL," Nitschke began to fulfill the vision.

WHAT DOES VISIONARY LEADERSHIP LOOK LIKE?

As a young man in his twenties, Vince Lombardi didn't know what he wanted to do with his life. A priest? A debt collector? A meat cutter like his father? A lawyer? None of those careers fit who Vince Lombardi was. It was only when his old teammate Andy Palau hired him as an assistant coach at St. Cecilia that Vince Lombardi discovered a fitting vision for his life: he would lead, he would teach, and he would coach.

Over time, Lombardi realized the importance of visionary leadership in every aspect of life. By the time he came to Green Bay, he had a clear vision of where he wanted to lead the team. He laid out his vision before the team and then led his players into the Promised Land of that vision. From studying Vince Lombardi's leadership life, we can see what authentic visionary leadership really looks like:

1. A visionary leader defines the ultimate goal. The leader describes what winning looks like, so that when the goal has been achieved, the team knows it's time to uncork the champagne. The leader's vision is optimistic, inspiring, and exciting. When the leader describes his or her vision to the team, everyone wants to help turn that vision into a reality.

To this day, quarterback Bart Starr remembers what Vince Lombardi told his players at their first team meeting in 1959: "Gentlemen, we're going to relentlessly chase perfection." Lombardi acknowledged that it was not possible to attain absolute perfection, but in the process of pursuing perfection, he said, "We will catch excellence."

As soon as that first meeting was over, Starr phoned his wife, Cherry, and told her that the Packers were going to win a lot of games in the coming season. Though it had only been a few months since the end of the humiliating 1-10-1 season, Bart Starr had a vision of a winning season ahead. Coach Lombardi planted that vision in his mind, and it was a vision that would soon be fulfilled.[20]

One of Coach Lombardi's biggest fans is John Madden, former NFL coach and longtime broadcaster, who coached the Oakland Raiders to victory in Super Bowl XI. Madden told me, "Vision is the difference maker when it comes to coaching. Everybody does the same thing as a coach. You have the same number of players, practices, timeouts, and so on. The big difference between Vince Lombardi and other coaches was his ability to know what the end is meant to look like. He laid the foundation at Green Bay, and he knew exactly what he wanted to build on that foundation. If you have a vision of the final product, if you know what it's supposed to look like, then you'll know that you've achieved it when you get there. Vince Lombardi was a visionary."

2. A visionary leader overcomes the natural inertia of the organization. People are, by nature, resistant to change. Most people would rather remain in a situation that is uncomfortable yet familiar than try something new and unfamiliar, even if the new experience means great rewards. Change makes people uncomfortable and demands more from them, so people resist change. The visionary leader's job is to cast a vision that is so powerful and so appealing that it overcomes the team's natural inertia and resistance to change.

When Vince Lombardi took over as head coach of the Green Bay Packers, he brought enormous change to the organization. He was going to demand extreme effort and focus from the players. Practices would be punishing. Discipline would be strict. Players would be 100 percent committed—or be cut. But Lombardi gave them a vision of what they would achieve if they would cooperate with the changes he imposed: The Packers would become a proud, winning organization again. When a team or organization believes there is celebration and success in their future, they will welcome and embrace change.

3. A visionary leader imparts a sense of purpose and identity to the team or organization. The leader's vision tells people who they are, why they exist as a team, and where they are going. The vision also motivates and energizes them for the journey.

Lieutenant Colonel Belinda L. Buckman of the United States Army wrote a paper on Coach Lombardi for the Army War College in Carlisle, Pennsylvania. In that paper, "Vince Lombardi as a Strategic Leader," Colonel Buckman wrote that the *War College Strategic Leadership Primer* states that the ability to formulate and communicate a strategic vision is probably a leader's "single most important contribution to the organization." Vision, she said, is "the leader-focused, organizational process that gives the organization its sense of purpose, direction, energy and identity."

Upon his arrival as head coach of the Green Bay Packers, Lombardi took command of an organization that had lost its sense of purpose, no longer saw itself as a winning organization, and had long ago lost its motivation to excel. Colonel Buckman observed that Coach Lombardi infused the dispirited Packers with his strategic vision and will to win by telling them that they would soon become "the New York Yankees of football." And, over the next few seasons, that's exactly what the Packers became.[21]

4. A visionary leader helps the team focus on what's important. A vision of the future focuses everyone's attention on the steps needed to achieve that vision. When an organization loses its focus and sense of direction, it's usually because people have lost sight of the organizational vision. A visionary leader keeps the vision uppermost in the minds of the players. The most effective leaders accomplish this by keeping the vision and processes simple.

Colonel Buckman observed that when Coach Lombardi arrived in Green Bay, most NFL coaches had a playbook that was at least four inches thick. Lombardi's playbook was slim—just an inch and a half thick. His goal was to simplify the game by teaching his players a system that involved fewer plays but with many options for each play. Lombardi reasoned that the quarterback on the field could read the defense and select the best option far more effectively than the coach on the sideline. Lombardi had learned this philosophy from his West Point mentor, Red Blaik. By eliminating complexity, Lombardi eliminated confusion and enabled his players to concentrate on refining the things they did best.[22]

5. A visionary leader invents and shapes the future of the organization. In books on leadership, you will often see *vision* defined as "the ability to see into the future" (or words to that effect). I disagree. No one can foretell the future—but great visionary leaders can *make the future happen*.

Visionary leaders don't merely study trends—they set trends. They don't try to anticipate change—they propel change. They don't rely on focus groups to tell them what they should do—their instinct and intuition tells them that. Visionary leaders look within to find the direction of the future—because they themselves are going to shape the future.

Vision is imagination married to action. Vision is a daydream that rolls up its sleeves and gets to work. Vince Lombardi was a visionary leader because he not only dreamed of a better future for the Packers and announced a better future for the Packers, but he also worked day and night to turn that dream into a reality. He invented the future with his own unstoppable efforts.

So learn the lessons of visionary leadership from the greatest football coach of all time. Before you begin leading, make sure you know where you are leading your team. Make sure you have a vision that inspires and motivates your people. Make sure you know what the end result looks like so that your people will know when it's time to celebrate.

Then focus on your vision, stay true to your vision, and watch your team turn your vision into a reality. The First Side of Leadership is Vision—and Coach Vince Lombardi was a role model of visionary leadership.

CHAPTER 2

THE COMMUNICATION SKILLS OF VINCE LOMBARDI

Leadership is based on a spiritual quality—the power to inspire, the power to inspire others to follow.
—**Vince Lombardi**

As head coach of the Green Bay Packers, Vince Lombardi worked with one of the legendary quarterbacks of the game, Bart Starr. Though Starr didn't come into the NFL as a highly recruited quarterback (he was selected 200th overall in the 1956 NFL draft), he finished his career with the then-league-best pass completion percentage (57.4) and then-second-best career passer rating (80.5). Though Lombardi built the Packers offense around the running game, Bart Starr's skills enabled Lombardi to switch to the aerial game at will.

The central feature of the Packers ground game was the Sweep. Before Lombardi devised the Packers Sweep, coaches would call a pre-designed play, and that play would require the blockers to hit a pre-designated spot and open a hole for the running back to run through. If the blockers failed to open a hole at that spot, the running back would usually be stopped for a loss or no gain. The genius of the Packers Sweep was its simplicity and flexibility. No longer were players locked into a rigid play design. They could respond instantly to changing conditions and new opportunities.

In the Packers Sweep, the offensive line seals off a corridor for the running back. The two guards form the outside wall of the running corridor, and the center and tackle on the running side form the inner wall of the corridor. The fullback leads the way into the corridor to block out any defenders who penetrate the walls. Meanwhile, the quarterback pitches the ball to the halfback, who follows the fullback into the running corridor.

As the blockers push back against the defenders, a hole will open up. When that hole opens up, the halfback will see daylight. Lombardi's instructions to the ball carrier are the soul of simplicity: "Run to daylight!" The ball carrier simply cuts back behind the wall of blockers and runs to the opening where daylight shines through. If all 11 players do their jobs, thinking and performing as one, then the ball carrier will usually be able to roll up a lot of yardage before he's taken down.

The Packers Sweep is not an "ace in the hole" play. Lombardi called it a "bread and butter" play—a play that would be used many times in any given game. The Packers rehearsed it endlessly. Guard Fuzzy Thurston once said, "I bet we ran that play no less than fifty times a day. There were so many variables . . . and Coach Lombardi was going to make sure we were sharp at all times."[23]

There was nothing secret about the Packers Sweep. It was the team's trademark, and opponents knew it was coming—again and again. But because of the adaptable, unpredictable "run-to-daylight" nature of the play, there was little an opponent could do to defend against it. The Sweep didn't follow a rigid pre-designed diagram each time. It unfolded differently according to the different defensive schemes opponents threw against it.

Lombardi once said of the Sweep, "There's nothing spectacular about it. It's just a yard-gainer . . . One of the advantages of this play is that we feel we can run it against any defense, even or odd."[24] And the way Coach Lombardi taught the Packers Sweep to his players was through that memorable, visual phrase: "Run to daylight."

I interviewed one of Coach Lombardi's earliest players, Andy Lukac, who played halfback (offense and defense) at Fordham, 1948 through 1950, when Lombardi was an assistant there. Andy later went on to a successful career as a high school football coach at St. Michael's in Union City, New Jersey.

"Here's the story on Vince Lombardi's famous 'run to daylight' saying," Andy told me. "Our practice facility had poor lighting to begin with. When our fullback Larry Higgins ran to the left he'd stumble and fall. Coach Lombardi would yell, 'You look like an old lady out there!' But when he ran to the right, Larry was terrific. He looked like an All-American.

"One day Coach asked Larry what made such a difference. Larry pointed to the left at a botanical garden with big hedges. He said, 'It's so dark over there, I can't see anything.' Then he pointed to the right, at a big white building in the sunlight. 'When I run that way,' he said, 'I can see perfectly.'

"So Coach Lombardi said, 'I get it. You run to daylight.' I was in the backfield at that moment, listening to Lombardi and Higgins, and I heard Coach say those exact words. That catchphrase, 'Run to daylight,' followed Coach Lombardi throughout his coaching career."

Vince Lombardi had a gift for the well-turned phrase. In addition to "Run to daylight," other memorable phrases attributed to Lombardi include: "Winners never quit, and quitters never win." "Once you learn to quit, it becomes a habit." "Show me a good loser, and I'll show you a loser." "If you aren't fired with enthusiasm, you will be fired with enthusiasm." "Perfection is unattainable, but if we chase perfection, we can catch excellence." "It's not whether you get knocked down, it's whether you get up." "Hurt is in the mind." "Leaders aren't born; they're made."

Andy Lukac had the privilege of being present when a then-unknown Vince Lombardi coined some of the most enduring phrases in the history of the game. Vince Lombardi was a great leader in large part because he was a skilled practitioner of The Second Side of Leadership: Communication.

LOMBARDI'S CHARISMA

Vince Lombardi was one of the great leadership communicators of all time, in any field. As a public speaker, he spoke confidently, without notes, and possessed a charismatic speaking style. He was a well-read leader and a clear thinker who expressed himself in simple, direct, everyday language. He was easy to follow and enjoyable to listen to. He was a storyteller. His working-class Brooklyn accent helped to conceal his keen, highly educated intellect, and enabled him to come across as what he truly was—a man of the people.

Lombardi's charisma and communication skills prompted Republican presidential candidate Richard Nixon to seriously investigate him as a potential running mate. Nixon, who had played football in high school and college, loved both football and leadership, and in 1968 he sent one of his campaign aides, John Mitchell, to investigate the possibility of a Nixon–Lombardi ticket. Mitchell returned with the disappointing news that Lombardi, a culturally conservative Democrat and a Catholic, was a Robert F. Kennedy supporter.[25]

Though Lombardi never got involved in politics, his fame and his communication skills made him a sought-after public speaker. He motivated audiences of businesspeople and civic leaders in pretty much the same way he motivated his teams—by speaking persuasively about leadership, success, character, faith, and individual responsibility.

His son, Vince Lombardi Jr., told me, "My dad was often wrong but never in doubt. When he got in front of people to speak, he was selling a message. He had a strong belief in the message he was selling, and he was absolutely convinced it would work. Dad had a charisma about him, and in a meeting you didn't doubt him. He was sold on the fact that his plans were right—and his absolute confidence may have been his greatest strength. Dad saw coaching as a salesmanship. His philosophy was, 'We are going to do it my way, and it'll work.'"

As a tight end with the Bears, Eagles, and Cowboys, Mike Ditka's playing career largely coincided with the Lombardi Era. Though Ditka was never coached by Vince Lombardi, he faced the Lombardi-coached Packers many times. His Hall of Fame career included three Super Bowl victories, one as a player and two as coach. He told me, "Vince Lombardi had great drive and confidence. He was a leader of men and he had a goal for his teams and a method of getting there. And he knew how to communicate it to his players and to audiences. One night, he was addressing a group of business leaders in New York City. He said, 'It's about time this country began to stand up and cheer for the doers and achievers, the winners in life.' Lombardi was also a great public speaker who never shied away from communicating his values and beliefs."

Wide receiver Boyd Dowler claimed that Coach Lombardi's communication skills made it easy to play for him. Lombardi? *Easy* to play for? But as Dowler explained it to Packers historian Royce Boyles, it makes a lot of sense. Royce told me, "Boyd said that Lombardi's preparation was so thorough, his communication so clear, you never had to guess as to what he expected of you. You always knew what he wanted, and that made everything simple. Boyd told me, 'Lombardi was easy to play for. If you had the ability, if you were good enough, then you didn't let him down. If you weren't a good player, you weren't gonna be there anyway. So it became easy. If you understood what you were supposed to do, and you went about doing it, you didn't have a lot of problems.'"

Clear communication is essential to great leadership. If you communicate well, your people will find you easy to follow. As I have studied Coach Lombardi's example and talked to people who knew him, I've discovered a number of communication principles that I have added to my own collection of public speaking insights. Here are some of Vince Lombardi's principles of leadership communication:

1. CULTIVATE A VOICE THAT COMMANDS ATTENTION.

New York Times columnist Dave Anderson told me, "Part of Vince Lombardi's mystique was his voice. He could growl at you and you'd never forget it."

Anderson recalled an incident that occurred after Packers star halfback Paul Hornung was suspended by the NFL in 1963 for betting on games. Hornung was repentant, and the league reinstated him in time for him to play the entire 1964 season. "Right after Hornung was reinstated," Anderson told me, "I went to Green Bay to hang out with him for a few days and write a major piece. Lunch at Saint Norbert's was served at noon on the dot. Hornung, Max McGee, and I got there late and ended up last in line at the cafeteria. We got our food and sat down to eat.

"I looked around and saw Vince Lombardi eating lunch a few tables away. When Lombardi had finished, he got up, walked toward Hornung and McGee, and stood behind them, breathing down their necks. He pointed to the big clock on the wall, then—in a voice you could hear all over the cafeteria—he said, 'You're supposed to be here at twelve, not ten after!' He let them know he wasn't happy. I'll never forget that voice. You could hear it a mile away."

Wide receiver Bob Schnelker played for Vince Lombardi with the New York Giants and was later an assistant to Lombardi with the Green Bay Packers. "Lombardi had a great speaking voice and a fine vocabulary—maybe because he had studied to be an attorney. He had a voice that demanded attention, and he used the power of his voice to get through to you and teach you what you needed to know. I always thought his physical presence helped, too. Solid."

Phil Vandersea played on the Packers defense for three seasons, beginning in 1966. He told me, "Coach Lombardi had great charisma, great personal presence, and he knew how to use it as a leader. The power of his voice was amazing, and we knew he was always in charge." And Charley Taylor, a wide receiver with the Redskins, was part of the last team Lombardi coached. Taylor told me, "The year and a half I spent with Coach Lombardi was great. He had a way about him. When he walked into a meeting room, you knew he was there. His voice would fill the place."

How do you cultivate a voice that commands attention—especially if you don't have a naturally powerful voice to begin with? A powerful voice begins with exercise. Your larynx or "voice box" is made of cartilage, nerves, and muscles—lots of muscles. The intrinsic laryngeal muscles are responsible for controlling sound production. These muscles include the cricothyroid muscle (which makes the vocal folds either tense or slack), the lateral and posterior cricoarytenoid muscles (which help shape the vocal chamber), the transverse and oblique arytenoid muscles (which constrict the vocal chamber and change the resonance of the voice), and the thyroarytenoid muscles (which lower the pitch of the voice). By exercising these muscles, you can help put more depth, power, and authority into your voice.

World-renowned speaking coach Bert Decker, the founder of Decker Communications, Inc., has trained politicians, business leaders, preachers, and coaches to speak with a more commanding voice. He recommends a simple but effective vocal exercise called "King Kong." Practice it daily for long-term improvement, and run through this exercise a few times privately ten to 30 minutes before you go before an audience. It works. Simply repeat the following phrase in a singing voice: "King Kong, Ding Dong, Bing Bong." The piano notes that correspond to the words are:

King	Kong,	Ding	Dong,	Bing	Bong
C	G	A	E	G	E-D-C

Sing that line once, then step it down a note lower and repeat, then step it down still lower and repeat. With each repetition, you are stretching the muscles and enlarging the chamber of your voice box—and you are deepening your voice. You'll find that your speaking voice is more resonant, more confident sounding, and more authoritative. By practicing this simple exercise before you speak, you'll be able to project a more persuasive and competent impression to your listeners.

When you speak, stand up straight, take deep breaths, relax, and speak from your diaphragm. When you fill your lungs with air, and use your diaphragm to push the air through your vocal system, your voice sounds stronger, steadier, and more powerful. Your voice won't crack or quaver if you speak from your diaphragm.

In the last minute or so before you speak, pause to focus and clear all distractions from your mind. Breathe steadily and deeply to draw oxygen into your bloodstream. This helps to fire up your brain for action. Pray, meditate, and fill your mind with positive, confident thoughts.

Above all, be yourself. Do you have a regional accent? Don't try to hide it—flaunt it. Pepper your speech with distinctive sayings and phrases from "the old neighborhood." Your accent makes you colorful and memorable. Vince Lombardi never tried to hide his Brooklyn accent—he reveled in it. (For some examples, search "Vince Lombardi" on YouTube and watch some videos of Coach Lombardi talking about leadership or football strategy—and notice how comfortable he is with his accent.)

Be confident, be authoritative, and take charge of the room. Everyone has come to hear what you have to say, so say it like you mean it. That's the Lombardi way of communicating.

2. COMMUNICATE CLEARLY AND SIMPLY.

Coach Lombardi opened every training camp by holding up a football and saying, "Gentlemen, this is a football." The first time Lombardi said that in a Packers meeting, wide receiver Max McGee piped up, "Uh, Coach, could you slow down a little? You're going too fast for us."[26]

Vince Lombardi took nothing for granted. Every year, he laid the basic foundation anew, and then he built on that foundation to teach his players the tactics, strategies, and principles that would yield a championship season. Lombardi never assumed his players knew what they needed to know. He treated them as blank slates, and he wrote on their slates, line upon line, precept upon precept.

As leaders, we should always start by laying the foundation, then building on that foundation, day by day, week by week. As Bart Starr told me, "Coach Lombardi was thorough, and he taught the team in basic terms. We had to function together as a unit, so he made sure we were all up-to-speed at all times. He communicated simply and he communicated well, so our assignments were always clear."

John Madden told me, "Vince Lombardi was everyone's coaching idol because he was so knowledgeable, and he explained everything so clearly. When I was twenty-five or twenty-six years old, I was a young coach at Allan Hancock College in Santa Maria, California. I thought I knew everything there was to know about football. One day, I heard that Vince Lombardi was going to hold a day-long coaching clinic at the University of Nevada, Reno. So I went out there and sat in the back row, just like when you go to church.

"Well, Coach Lombardi blew me away! I thought I knew all this stuff, but he spent *eight hours* teaching the Packers Sweep! Eight hours! I realized then that I knew nothing. Sid Gillman, the veteran NFL coach, was sitting up in the front row. I figured, 'Hey, if Gillman is up there, I'd better move up front, too.' So at the next break, I moved as close to the front of the room as I could get.

"At that point, I could talk for maybe two or three minutes on a play, but eight hours on one play! Even though he went into detail, he kept it clear and simple. *Every little thing* Lombardi taught that day had a purpose. He was a big advocate of sound technique, so he would go in-depth on each player's assignment. He'd break it down and show you the precise techniques each player had to master in order for the play to work.

"One thing Coach Lombardi said at the Reno clinic: 'We're going to practice the Sweep more and longer than you're going to practice trying to stop it. And we're going to execute it better than you can execute any defensive play to stop it. And we're going to run it again and again until you figure out a way to stop us, which will probably never happen.' Vince Lombardi believed that every team needed a signature play to rely on to guarantee yardage when they needed it. The Sweep was Lombardi's signature play.

"The Sweep was basic and fundamental, and Lombardi believed that you win by mastering the fundamentals. He said, 'Football is only two things—blocking and tackling.' He didn't have a thick playbook. He had a few simple plays that could be run in a variety of ways, with a lot of options. He made sure his teams could run those plays in their sleep. When I realized that Lombardi was great because he kept everything clear and simple, a light went on in my head. Young coaches want to show off their brilliance, so they tend to focus too much on X's and O's. Lombardi's 'keep-it-simple' philosophy showed me I needed to teach my players to master the fundamentals. He taught me that you win by doing simple things consistently well—not by doing complicated things poorly."

Former Redskins quarterback Sonny Jurgensen played 18 seasons in the NFL, including the 1969 season under Coach Lombardi. Jurgensen told me, "I've studied three of the winningest coaches of all time—Vince Lombardi, John Wooden of the UCLA Bruins, and Red Auerbach of the Boston Celtics. They all had one thing in common: They simplified the game and didn't try to complicate things. John Havlicek once told me the Celtics only had six plays and they won eleven NBA titles. Vince Lombardi believed winning was all about executing the fundamentals, and he had the ability to get that across to his players."

Sometimes Coach Lombardi got carried away and overcoached his players. Ken Bowman, who played center during the Packers' glory years, told me that when Lombardi realized he'd gone too far, he would simplify his communication with the team in order to get his players to relax and play to the best of their ability. "On the weeks we were to play a weak opponent," Bowman said, "Lombardi worked us extra-hard. He wanted to make sure we didn't become overconfident and slack off. We'd be in pads and hitting every day, and by game day we were so beat up and exhausted, it was all we could do to limp into the stadium.

"One Sunday, we were losing a game we should have been winning with ease. In fact, by halftime, we were down 21 to zero. We went into the locker room thinking Coach Lombardi was going to be ready to kill us all. Instead, we found him sitting calmly at a table in the middle of the room.

"Very soft-spoken, he said, 'Boys, I want to tell you a story. Last night, I was reading my Bible.' Then he turned to Paul Hornung, who had a bit of a wild streak, and he said, 'You ought to read the Bible someday, Paul. Lots of good stuff in there.' We all laughed, and Coach said, 'I was reading St. Paul's first letter to the Corinthians. He wrote, 'Don't you know that those who run in a race all run, but only one receives the prize? Run in such a way that you may win the crown.'[27] That's the reputation of the Green Bay Packers, going all the way back to the days of Curly Lambeau. All I ask is that you go out there and uphold that tradition.'

"It was the best halftime speech I had ever heard. We went out and won the game, 28 to 21. Coach Lombardi knew he'd overworked us, but that simple, straight-from-the-heart speech gave us the shot of adrenaline we needed. He knew how to say the right thing at the right time."

Boyd Dowler, who was Green Bay's star wide receiver for 11 seasons, recalls that Coach Lombardi communicated with clarity by setting clear expectations for every member of the team. Dowler told me, "Vince Lombardi would stand up, look you right in the eye, and tell you what he expected from you. In fact, he'd tell you what would happen before it happened, if you did things his way. He'd never lie to you. Lombardi would say: 'If you do what I ask of you, we'll win together.' And it always worked out exactly as he said it would. But if you insisted on pursuing individual glory instead of being part of the team, you wouldn't be a Packer for very long. Lombardi knew very early that we had the right material—and we all knew we had the right coach. We had everything we needed to win if we did things his way."

3. MAINTAIN YOUR SENSE OF HUMOR— ESPECIALLY IN TENSE SITUATIONS.

Actor Dan Lauria was highly acclaimed for his portrayal of Coach Lombardi in the 2010 Broadway production *Lombardi*, based on the David Maraniss book *When Pride Still Mattered*. Lauria meticulously researched the role and interviewed many of Coach Lombardi's former players, asking them what they would most want to see in his portrayal of their coach. "More than one emphasized the coach's sense of humor," Lauria said, adding that Lombardi "had a great laugh and liked to kid around, especially the Saturday before a game. The work had been done and the game plan was in place. He liked the players to stay loose."

Lauria noted that his conversations with Lombardi's star players seemed to follow a consistent pattern. "They'd go into a humorous story, but eventually they'd all be in tears. Willie Wood could not go one minute without crying. They all had great stories."

One of the details that was recounted to Dan Lauria again and again was the way Coach Lombardi's wife Marie would use humor to defuse her husband's irascible temper. If the Lombardis were out in public together and Vince would become angry and start ranting, Marie would raise her pinkie finger as a signal. Without a word, Lombardi understood that he was making a fool of himself—he'd shut up, lock pinkies with Marie, and his tantrum was over.

Lauria raised the pinkie-locking ritual when he interviewed Sonny Jurgensen—and Sonny instantly became emotional. Choking back tears, Jurgensen said that the pinkie-lock was more than just a funny ritual to defuse the tension. It was an expression of love between Vince and Marie—and Jurgensen saw it take place many times after Vince was diagnosed with terminal cancer. He told Lauria, "I would take Marie to the hospital to see him . . . and as soon as they saw each other, they'd lock pinkies."[28]

Pat Peppler was the Packers' director of player personnel under Vince Lombardi and later worked in front office and coaching roles with several NFL teams. He was 91 when I interviewed him, and his memories of Coach Lombardi were as fresh as this morning's news. Peppler vividly recalled Lombardi's quick humor.

"Vince went from high school coaching into the college ranks," Peppler told me. "He ended up at Army as an assistant to Red Blaik. Vince respected the discipline at Army. In those days, Blaik would send his assistants into New York City for a football meeting with the Army generals. Those generals could be tough, and they were always second-guessing the coaching decisions. So one guy started in on

Lombardi, saying, 'Why are you playing Ray Malavasi at nose tackle? Is it because he's Italian?' Vince started to lose his temper, but then he composed himself and said, 'General, I'm not playing Malavasi because *he's* Italian. I'm playing him because *I'm* Italian!'"

As we will later see, the military leader Lombardi said that to was probably General Douglas MacArthur—and Lombardi got away with it. A quick wit will take you a lot farther than a quick temper.

4. TO BE A GREAT LEADER, BE A TEACHER.

Longtime college football coach Bill Curry had a decade-long career as a center in the NFL, including two years with the Packers (1965–1966). He told me, "I learned from Vince Lombardi that in order to be a great leader, it is necessary to take people to places they don't want to go. Lombardi knew how to do that. He had a passion for the game that was off the charts. He could walk into a room and change the atmosphere without saying a word. And when he spoke, everybody listened.

"Vince Lombardi was a great teacher. In fact, he was a high school physics teacher, so he taught by memorization and repetition. If you were around Coach Lombardi for three days, he could get in your hard drive forever. Whatever he taught you, you'd never forget."

Quarterback Bart Starr agrees. He told me, "Vince Lombardi was an exceptional teacher who was well prepared for every classroom session. That transferred to each player. He prepared us as thoroughly, whether we were going out on the practice field or going out to play a crucial game. We all learned so much from Vince Lombardi."

Wide receiver Bob Long, who played for Coach Lombardi in both Green Bay and Washington, told me, "Vince Lombardi was a teacher first. He'd roll out a big black board on the practice field and diagram a play. An hour and a half later, he'd still be teaching the same play. It was like you were back in high school."

Zeke Bratkowski was a backup quarterback to Bart Starr. After Starr was injured in the 1965 Western Division championship game, Bratkowski subbed in and led the Packers to a 13-10 victory over the Baltimore Colts. He told me, "Vince Lombardi was a great teacher. He could take a play apart and then put it back together again. He was especially detail-oriented with the quarterbacks. When he spoke to Bart and me during the week, he'd say, 'Make a note of this.' And we'd write down whatever he told us, like a student taking notes in school. Then, on Saturday, Bart and I would go over all of the notes we took. Coach Lombardi prepared us well during the week, and then on Sunday, during the games, he'd give us total leeway on audibles. He'd never second-guess us."

Columnist Dave Anderson told me, "I believe the best coaches are also the best teachers. Vince Lombardi had a background as a teacher. At Saint Cecilia High School in New Jersey, he coached football and basketball and taught Latin and other of subjects. It's clear that being an experienced teacher made him a better coach. Lombardi was a tough coach because he was a tough teacher. Isn't it interesting that the teachers we remember most are those who were strict and demanding but also great communicators? That's the kind of teacher Vince Lombardi was. That's why, as tough as he was, he's remembered with such fondness."

Lombardi's biographer, David Maraniss, told me, "From his early days as a high school teacher in New Jersey all the way through his NFL career, Vince Lombardi was a great teacher. He had the capacity to take complex ideas and simplify them so that his players knew exactly what to do during games. Along with that, Lombardi believed in absolute preparation. He'd run his drills over and over again so that they became second nature to the players. As a result, the game actually seemed to slow down for his players, compared with the intensity of the practices. With that kind of discipline, the Packers developed freedom on the field—the freedom to play instinctively, without having to think about each step. Lombardi's philosophy was to teach the basics first, and then the freedom would follow."

Vince Lombardi was not just a rousing speaker who gave fiery locker room speeches. He was a mentor who tailored his leadership approach to the needs of each individual player on the team. Former Redskins quarterback Sonny Jurgensen told me, "Vince Lombardi had great skills as a communicator, and he didn't communicate the same way with all his players. He knew the best way to get through to each guy."

Lombardi was skilled at communicating his vision in such a way that his players could see what he saw in their own minds. He intuitively understood the wisdom of Aristotle, who said, "The soul never thinks without a picture." As former Packers defensive end Willie Davis told me, "Coach Lombardi taught football and life in a way that helped you picture it in your mind. When he spoke, you could visualize doing what he said. You thought, 'I can do this and become successful with it.'"

One observation I heard again and again from Coach Lombardi's players was that he didn't just coach football—he taught life skills. He instructed his players in how to be successful not only on the football field, but in all their future endeavors.

Pat Richter, who played his entire career with the Washington Redskins, told me, "Vince Lombardi had a quote on his desk: 'The greatness of a loss is not so much what is lost but what is left.' He was saying, in effect, 'Can you come back after a setback in life? Can you push your way through obstacles and be successful long after your football days are over?'

"Coach Lombardi kept driving us to practice professionalism. He often said, 'You can't have a careless attitude, or this enterprise will not be successful.' He was telling us that, long after our NFL careers for over, we should act with professionalism toward our work, our families, our financial responsibilities, and everything else in life."

Former Packers defensive tackle Jim Weatherwax told me, "After I retired from football, I operated a restaurant in California and used Vince Lombardi's leadership principles to run my business. I don't know how I would have succeeded without his influence. Everyone on the team learned life lessons from him. He was a great teacher."

In *Pillars of the NFL*, Chicago Bears executive Patrick McCaskey describes the hard-nosed teaching style of Vince Lombardi:

> He stands looking out in his sunglasses, white football pants with black belt, and white cotton shirt. As the sun beats down, he takes his Green Bay Packers cap off, wipes his forehead, and puts his cap back on . . . He bellows out to one of his linemen: "You turkey. Look at that sloppy stance." . . . The drill continues mercilessly. Finally, the coach sees some improvement. He shakes his head to himself and his mood changes. He turns away and chuckles quietly . . .
>
> For Lombardi, this is when games are won or lost. No one is as demanding as Lombardi. No one wins like him either . . .

Over the course of training camp, Lombardi will beat down his players. He will constantly challenge their endurance. He will drill them a thousand times on every play, instruct them on every move they must make. And just when his players are ready to explode, he will praise them and acknowledge their achievements.[29]

Vince Lombardi's son, Vince Jr., is a motivational speaker who has written books on his father's coaching style and leadership philosophy. In *The Lombardi Rules*, Vince Jr. observed that his father used the terms *coaching* and *teaching* interchangeably. He writes:

As both a teacher and a coach, Lombardi concentrated on the *whys*. "I never tell a player, 'This is my way, now do it,'" he once said. "Instead, I say, 'This is the way we do it, and this is why we do it.'" . . .

Lombardi taught to the bottom of the "class," going slowly enough—and being repetitive enough—so that *no one* was left behind . . . The risk in this style of teaching/coaching, of course, is that the top of the class—or even the teacher—will get bored. Lombardi avoided this in part by the simple force of his personality and convictions. He had a way of making even a routine task sound important, as if there *were* no routine tasks . . .

"I loved it," recalled Packers quarterback Bart Starr. "I never, ever was bored or tired at any meeting we were in with Lombardi. I appreciated what he was trying to teach. He was always trying to raise the bar."[30]

Great leaders must be great communicators—and great communicators must be great teachers.

5. COMMUNICATE ENTHUSIASM!

Jerry Kramer enjoyed an 11-year career as an offensive lineman with the Green Bay Packers and was one of the dependable anchormen of the Packers Sweep. He told me, "Coach Lombardi was a dynamo of enthusiasm. I can still hear his voice in my mind—'We're gonna have a great practice today!' Or he'd tell us, 'What a terrific game we have coming up on Sunday!' And we believed it, we felt it in our bones! A lot of coaches will say that kind of thing, and everybody just says, 'Sure, Coach, whatever you say.' It just rings hollow. But if Coach Lombardi said it, you knew he meant it. He was fired up, and that got us all fired up. His enthusiasm was infectious. He got us to play with intensity by the power of his voice and his emotions."

Ruth Pitts Litman is the widow of halfback Elijah Pitts, who played for Lombardi in Green Bay and scored two touchdowns in Super Bowl I. He passed away in 1997. Ruth recalled how inspired and motivated her husband felt after one of Coach Lombardi's speeches. "Coach Lombardi was one of the outstanding motivators of his time," she told me. "Elijah once said to me, 'After his speech before our game today, I was so ready to play that I could have put a hole through the locker room wall with my fist.' My husband told me that Coach Lombardi was always teaching his players to have pride in who they were, pride in performance, pride in their character and discipline. Coach Lombardi inspired them with enthusiasm. Elijah was a special man, and Coach Lombardi's influence made him even stronger."

Communicating enthusiasm is a key challenge for leaders in any field, whether in sports or business or the church. When people know their leader is passionate about winning, they'll be motivated to play their game with eagerness and intensity. A leader who communicates enthusiasm also communicates confidence. Enthusiasm is a form of optimism and self-assurance. An enthusiastic leader conveys a can-do attitude to the troops. Enthusiasm is contagious—and enthusiasm wins.

Longtime Packers publicist Chuck Lane told me, "Coach Lombardi had a huge influence on my life. He was emotional and he communicated his emotions to his players. When he got fired up, we all got fired up. He knew how to reach both the intellect and the emotions. He could teach, he could motivate, he could energize. He invented a concept he called 'heart power,' the ability to touch the emotions. Whether he was speaking to his players in the locker room or addressing an audience at a business luncheon, he went straight for the heart—and he reached it."

Willie Davis told me, "You could hear his voice from a block away, and when you heard it, you *felt* something. His emotion became our emotion. You could be exhausted, spent, unable to move—but then Coach Lombardi would start talking, and he'd get your blood pumping, and soon you were ready to go out and run your heart out for him. Emotion—he had it, and he communicated it to us."

Green Bay Packers historian Cliff Cristl told me, "Vince Lombardi would beat his players down early in the week, particularly if they had a weak opponent on Sunday. Then, by the end of the week, through positive reinforcement, he'd have his team ready to go. Lombardi realized that his players needed a mind-set of confidence and enthusiasm. His message was, 'Gentlemen, you are the Green

Bay Packers and you are expected to win. You're the best, so go out there and play that way.'"

Mary Jane Van Duyse Sorgel brings a unique perspective to Vince Lombardi as a leader and communicator. She was a fresh-faced, baton-twirling teenager when she first became associated with the Green Bay Packers. Her father owned a dance hall and roller rink in Sturgeon Bay, 45 miles northeast of Green Bay. One day in 1949, a man named Wilner Burke brought his Lumberjack Band to play at the dance hall—and the Lumberjack Band also happened to be the Packers band during football season.

"I was twirling my baton," Mary Jane told me, "and Wilner Burke saw me and said, 'Would you like to come and twirl on the Packers field next Sunday?' So with my mom's permission, I went and performed at the game. A couple of years later, Wilner made me a regular baton twirler and drum majorette with the band."

Mary Jane won a national baton-twirling contest in 1954 and performed in halftime shows during those tough years when the Packers went through a succession of coaches. She would also perform on TV and in personal appearances for the March of Dimes and other charities. On one occasion, while in Chicago with the Packers band, a Chicago sportswriter dubbed her "Green Bay's Golden Girl." Blond and decked out in a sparkling golden costume, she fit the moniker—and sportswriters found it easier to call her "The Golden Girl" than to remember how to spell "Van Duyse."

When Vince Lombardi arrived in 1959, he asked Mary Jane to assemble a cheerleading squad. By this time, Mary Jane ran a studio and taught dancing and baton-twirling, so she had a lot of talent to select from. Mary Jane was the choreographer and featured twirler, and the Packers cheerleaders became known as "Mary Jane and her Golden Girls." She worked directly with both Vince Lombardi and his wife Marie. Mrs. Lombardi designed green and gold outfits that complemented the players' uniforms.

Vince Lombardi continually communicated to Mary Jane how much he appreciated and valued the Golden Girls' contribution. "He was always so nice to me," Mary Jane recalled. "He treated me as part of the Packers organization, and after every performance, he'd flash a grin and say, 'Great job, Mary!' His approval meant so much.

"One time, the Packers band had a party, and Coach Lombardi got up in front of everybody and said, 'Mary, our band doesn't always get its lines straight, but who cares? Nobody's looking at the band—they are all looking at you!' Everybody got a kick out of that. But that was Vince Lombardi—he was always handing out compliments and making you feel good to be a part of everything. He was a charming man, and his wife Marie was a sweetheart. I still keep in touch with their daughter, Susan.

"Coach Lombardi was also in complete command and very strict. When he hollered, you'd move—yet you respected him and loved him. One Sunday, during the halftime show, we had the band on the field, going through its halftime routine—but the routine went long. So Lombardi came out and started yelling, 'Mary! Mary! Get that band off of the field! We're over-time, and you have to watch the clock!' I knew it was serious, because that was the loudest I'd ever heard him yell at me. So I dashed over to the band director, who was conducting from a ladder, and I said, 'Hurry! The team's coming out!' So the director picked up the tempo and got the band off the field in a hurry.

"Vince Lombardi was a perfectionist about every detail. Everything had to come off right on time. And he taught the rest of us to be perfectionists as well. I learned so much from him about being on time and doing all the little things that added up to excellence. He was always teaching, and I was always learning from him.

"If I had to compare the Packers organization to anything, I would compare it to a family. Vince and Marie Lombardi made us all feel included in this big family, and the atmosphere in that organization was unlike anything I've ever seen. When Vince Lombardi announced he was leaving the Packers, all of my Golden Girls and I were crying, it was so sad. When he left, the family atmosphere went with him.

"I was with the Packers for twenty-two years, and I still tell everyone what a great time that was in my life. I was really fortunate to be a part of the Packers organization during those championship years, and in a real sense, to be part of Vince Lombardi's family."

Vince Lombardi was no softie. He was a demanding leader who often got things done at the top of his lungs. But he earned the admiration of everyone from players to cheerleaders, because he communicated enthusiasm and energy—and yes, he communicated a family kind of love.

6. COMMUNICATE TO INSPIRE.

"Leadership," Coach Lombardi once said, "is based on a spiritual quality—the power to inspire, the power to inspire others to follow."[31] There have been few greater role models of inspirational leadership than Vince Lombardi.

Wide receiver Carroll Dale played for the Packers from 1965 to 1972. He told me, "Before the first Super Bowl, Coach Lombardi stressed to us that we were representing the entire NFL. His message was, 'Keep your mouth shut and go play.' In his pregame speeches, in fact in *all* his communication with the team, he knew when to push the right buttons and how to do it."

One of Lombardi's top assistants in Green Bay, Bob Schnelker, told me, "Lombardi had an incredible ability to know exactly when to give his team a pep talk. Sometimes the team needs it early in the week to get revved up for practice. Other times, the team needs a big emotional boost in the locker room just before the game. Lombardi always knew exactly the right moment, and he always had the right words to say to the players and assistant coaches."

The ability to know what to say and when to say it requires an exceptional level of sensitivity from a leader. You have to observe your people, watch their body language, and listen carefully to the words they say—including what they say to each other when they don't know you're listening. You have to pick up a vibe from your people—and you do this by training yourself to see, hear, and notice.

Inspirational "pep talks" should be used sparingly. If you fire up your people too often, your voice and words will lose their impact. You can only go to that well so often before it dries up. But if you observe carefully, and you notice those times when your people begin to sag and lose focus or approach a point of exhaustion, you'll be able to target the precise moment for a memorable, motivational word to your team.

The right word, delivered at the right time, will stick in the mind forever. Jerry Kramer recalls, "Coach Lombardi was famous for his sayings. We called them 'Lombardiisms.' My favorite Lombardi quote was, 'You don't do things right once in a while—you do them right all the time.' That's such an obvious notion, it sounds like a cliché—but it really stuck in my mind. Those words would come back to me whenever I was tempted to let down or slack off or take a shortcut. I'd hear those words in Coach Lombardi's raspy voice, and I'd think, 'No, I'm not going to slack off. I'm going to do this the right way, every time.' Sayings like that gave me an inspirational boost whenever I needed it, and they made me a better, more consistent player."

Great inspirational speeches don't have to be long. They just need to lift the spirit and ignite the emotions. Former Packers guard Bob Hyland told me, "Vince Lombardi was optimistic, and he transmitted hope and optimism to his players. He made you believe you could do anything, and the confidence he inspired in us enabled us to accomplish great things. That's the kind of coach you want to play for."

Former Packers tight end Dick Capp told me that Coach Lombardi always knew what kind of emotional boost he needed, whether a pat on the back or a kick in the pants. "Some coaches," he told me, "only try to inspire and motivate you on game day. Coach Lombardi would always give us a pep talk before practice to inspire us to give our best effort. The only way to be prepared on game day is to treat every practice like it's a game, like everything is on the line.

"Soon after I made the team, I was heading down the tunnel before the first game of the season. Coach Lombardi said to me, 'Hey, Dick, you look great in the green and gold!' At that moment, I felt seven feet tall. Coach Lombardi made me feel like a full-fledged member of the team.

"But there were times I needed a different kind of motivation. One day during practice, I kind of lost focus and dropped an easy pass. Coach Lombardi called out to me, 'Relax, Dick. If you don't make it here, I know a lot of coaches in the league. And get that face mask off so you can see the ball.' He was joking—but he was letting me know that I needed to make those catches or I might not be wearing the green and gold much longer.

"Coach Lombardi taught me to never let up until the game is over. You play the full sixty minutes with intensity. Late in the fourth quarter of Super Bowl II, we had two minutes left and we were up 33 to 14. There was no way the Raiders were going to get back into that game. With two minutes remaining, and the game essentially a done deal, we had to punt. I was on the special teams unit, and with a little extra effort, I probably could have downed the ball and pinned the Raiders deep in their own territory. But with such a big lead, I just let the ball bounce into the end zone for a touchback.

"When I got back to the sideline, Coach Lombardi got right in my face. He chewed me out for not trying to down the ball on the two. I thought about it, and I realized he was right. He was yelling at me to teach me something about effort: You never let up. You maintain your intensity and play it like you mean it until the clock runs out. It's a lesson I've carried with me ever since."

I mentioned that incident to Royce Boyles, and he said, "Isn't that amazing? Not only is that the last two minutes of the game, it's the last two minutes of Lombardi's Green Bay coaching career—yet there he is, getting on Dick Capp, a special teamer, trying to strengthen his work ethic. Lombardi wasn't just teaching football, he was teaching life. And he never let up."

Packers defensive tackle Ron Kostelnik was a major factor in the Packers' championships in Super Bowls I and II. He died in 1993 at age 53. I spoke with Kostelnik's widow, Peggy, and she told me a revealing story about Coach Lombardi's powers of persuasion—and his ability to communicate effectively even *without* words.

"Coach Lombardi had a natural charisma about him," she said. "When he spoke, his players listened—and they did what he said. During the winter months, the Packers players were often getting head colds. Coach Lombardi believed that exposure to the cold was a factor, so he told his players to start wearing hats when they went outside.

"Ron and I were very young, and we had just had a baby when he started playing in Green Bay. One day, we were out pushing the baby carriage when Vince Lombardi drove by. He spotted Ron and saw that he wasn't wearing a hat. Lombardi slowed down and didn't have to say a word. He just pointed to his head as he cruised by. Ron turned right around, went back to our little apartment, and came back a minute later wearing a hat. Then we continued our walk.

"That's the power of Vince Lombardi's personality. He cared about his players—and he was totally in charge. When he walked into a room, you felt his presence. The players respected him, and I know he respected them as well."

7. COMMUNICATE CERTAINTIES!

Though Bob Harlan was not with the Packers organization during the Lombardi era (he joined as assistant general manager in 1971), he is well acquainted with Packers legend and lore. He served as CEO of the Packers from 1989 to 2008, and now serves as a goodwill ambassador for the team. He is credited with spearheading the modernization of Lambeau Field and (along with general manager Ron Wolf) helping to restore the team to dominance in the Brett Favre–Reggie White era.

"Vince Lombardi inherited a terrible team," Harlan told me, "but he demanded full authority from the board and would not take no for an answer. He was totally in charge, and he made it clear that the Packers were going to start winning immediately. Though some would have you believe that Lombardi ruled by fear, what he really instilled in his players was respect. So many of his players, even fifty years later, say they still feel his influence on their lives. He helped them become great, not only as football players but as human beings. He shaped their futures in a powerful way. A leader couldn't ask for a richer legacy than that."

Great leaders are visionaries who have learned to communicate their vision in a commanding, compelling way. They communicate clearly and simply. They are teachers and mentors, patiently instructing, guiding, and correcting the people they lead. The best leaders are sensitive to the individual personality traits of their followers, and they tailor their communication style to each individual's needs. Great leaders communicate optimism and confidence to their followers. They communicate to inspire and motivate.

Every day in your leadership role, you must make a decision: Will I communicate optimism and hope today—or will I communicate pessimism and fear? Will I give my followers an inspiring vision to aim for—or will I leave them in the dark about the direction I'm taking them?

Communicate the vision with authority and enthusiasm. Don't merely express opinions—express certainties! Tell your people in no uncertain terms what they will achieve if they follow your leadership and carry out your vision. Authentic leaders inspire action, move organizations, and change the world through the power of their words.

"They call it coaching, but it is teaching," Lombardi once said. "You do not just tell them . . . You show them the reasons." So lead the Lombardi way. Be a communicator, be a teacher, and be a leader.

CHAPTER 3

THE PEOPLE SKILLS OF VINCE LOMBARDI

People who work together will win, whether it be against complex football defenses, or the problems of modern society.[32]
—Vince Lombardi

" One day in practice," Jerry Kramer told me, "I jumped off-side and Coach Lombardi got all over me. To Lombardi, mental errors were unacceptable, so he really lit into me.

"After practice, I dragged myself into the locker room and sat on the bench in front of my locker, feeling completely worthless. I was so far down, I thought, *I just can't please this man. There's nothing I can do to make him happy. I need to get traded to another team or maybe get out of football altogether.* I must have sat there in that mood for a good half hour.

"Coach Lombardi saw me from the far end of the locker room, and he came over and slapped me on the back and mussed up my hair. 'Jerry,' he said, 'one of these days, you're going to be the best guard in football.' Instantly, I felt I was ten feet tall. Those words changed my whole world.

"Lombardi's approach was important to all of us on the team. He knew what we needed. He'd push us and drive us until we were ready to give up on ourselves, on him, and on football—then he'd fill us up with pride and determination, and we were ready to run through walls for him again.

"Coach Lombardi was constantly yelling at Paul Hornung. Lombardi loved the guy, but he knew that Paul thrived on being yelled at. He knew that if he screamed at Hornung, his star running back—and Hornung accepted it—the other players would more readily accept Lombardi's tirades. Yet Coach Lombardi knew not to yell at his wide receiver, Max McGee, because Max couldn't take being called out in front of his teammates. He might lose his focus and his confidence if Lombardi embarrassed him in front of his teammates.

"Vince Lombardi was a master psychologist. He used a combination of approaches to motivate people and get them to perform. He always knew whether chewing a guy out or patting him on the back would produce the positive change he was looking for."

Jerry Kramer was one of a number of Packers players and assistants who referred to Vince Lombardi as a "master psychologist" or "great psychologist." Another was Steve Wright, offensive tackle with the Green Bay Packers from 1964 to 1968. He told me, "Coach Lombardi was a master psychologist. He knew each of us as individuals, and he didn't treat any two guys alike. He'd say, 'Here's a job. Get it done or get out of the way. If you can't do it, I've got ten other guys who can take your place.' He'd chew you up one side and down the other. Later, he'd put his arm around you and say, 'You're gonna do all right.' Coach knew what made each player tick and how to get the most out of each of us."

Jim Weatherwax was a defensive tackle for the Packers. Selected in the 1965 NFL draft, Weatherwax played three seasons with Green

Bay and was a member of the Super Bowl I Champion Packers and has the distinction of making the first official tackle in Super Bowl history. "Vince Lombardi knew people because he was a psychologist," Weatherwax told me. "He knew each one of us and how to get the best out of us. He worked at it and was always observing us closely, getting to know us as individuals. He knew exactly what motivated each of us, what he wanted out of each of us, and he didn't treat any two players the same."

Ken Bowman played center for the Green Bay Packers from 1964 to 1973. Like so many others, he told me, "Vince Lombardi was a great psychologist. He understood that what motivated one player might demoralize another. He was good at analyzing players, and he knew which players he could chew out and which players couldn't take it. He individualized his coaching techniques. He figured out that some players actually worked harder when they were mad at him—'I'll show that old so-and-so!' Other players played better because they wanted to please their beloved coach. Coach Lombardi inspired some players to love him, some to fear him, some to be mad—but whatever it took, he got each player to do his best. He had incredible skills as a motivator."

Running back Jim Grabowski played college football at the University of Illinois and was selected in the first round of the 1966 NFL draft by the Green Bay Packers (ninth selection overall). He was also the first overall pick that year in the AFL draft, selected by the Miami Dolphins. So Vince Lombardi found himself bidding against the Dolphins for Grabowski's services.

Grabowski told me, "The Packers flew me to Green Bay in a private plane, along with my attorney, Arthur Morse. Arthur told me, 'No matter what Lombardi says, tell him you need twenty-four hours to think it over.' So we got to the Packers facility, and they ushered us down this hallway with all of these championship pictures and into Coach Lombardi's office. It was a huge room, lined with trophies and photos, with a long boardroom table—very impressive. And there was Vince Lombardi. We sat across from him, and he looked us in the eye—very intimidating.

"Arthur said, 'Mr. Lombardi, you probably know that the Dolphins' offer is quite a bit more than yours.' And Lombardi looked at me and said, 'Jim, here's what we'll offer you.' And he laid out the Packers offer. For a twenty-year-old kid fresh out of college, it seemed like a huge pot-full of money. I completely forgot what my attorney had said about needing twenty-four hours to consider it. Without thinking, I said, 'Yes!' My attorney was fit to be tied—but Lombardi had won me over.

"Looking back, I realize that Vince Lombardi knew exactly what he was doing. He knew the impact all that Packers tradition and legend would have on a young player like me. He was a mastermind, a great psychologist."

Grabowski played five seasons for the Packers and one season for the Chicago Bears. He earned NFL championship rings in Super Bowls I and II and went on to a three-decade career in broadcasting.

Sportswriter and novelist W. C. Heinz was Coach Lombardi's writing partner on *Run to Daylight*. In a collection of his best sports columns, *The Top of His Game*, Heinz recalled sitting down with Lombardi for an hour and naming off all 36 players on the Packers roster. Every time Heinz named a player, Lombardi instantly gave him a thumbnail sketch of that player's personality, emotional makeup, skills, strengths, and weaknesses.

For example, when Heinz said the name of Packers defensive end Willie Davis, Lombardi said, "A hell of a young man. Very excitable under game conditions. A worrier. Before a game he's got that worried look, so I try to bolster his confidence. He's not worried about the team losing—he's got confidence in the team—but he's worried about how Willie Davis will perform . . . about not letting his team down. Fine brain, too. In Willie Davis, we got a great one."[33] Lombardi's encyclopedic knowledge of his players enabled him to find the precise combination of words and incentives to motivate their peak performances.

Don Horn joined the Packers in 1967 as a backup to Bart Starr. He told me, "I was amazed at Coach Lombardi's ability to know exactly when each individual needed a little extra motivation. For one player, it might be ten minutes prior to the game. For another, it might be a day or two before. Lombardi could read each of us, and he knew which ones were mentally ready to play. He also had an uncanny feel for the readiness of the team as a whole.

"One afternoon during my rookie year, we were preparing for a big game—I think it was the 49ers. Not too long into our practice, guys were making a lot of errors and mental mistakes. Finally, Coach Lombardi had had enough. He yelled, 'Get off my practice field and don't come back until you're ready to practice!' Then he walked off the field, got into his car, and drove off. We all just stared with our mouths open. Not sure what to do, we left the field and prepared for our scheduled team meetings later that day. We assembled, Lombardi showed up, and he had our full attention. The next day at practice, no one made a single mental mistake. And we won on Sunday as well."

There's something about the act of canceling a practice and walking away that shows that a coach means what he says. Sometimes it's hard to convey that level of seriousness to players without some sort of dramatic gesture. Sonny Jurgensen recalled that Lombardi had to use this same technique during his year with the Redskins.

Jurgensen called Lombardi "a great communicator" who was "able to convey what he wanted done." He recalled:

> Practices were an hour and a half, but if they weren't going right, he'd say, "Everybody in" and would send everybody off the field . . . We didn't know whether to get undressed and go back to the dorm or what . . . [The assistant coaches] said, "Just sit here in your uniforms and wait for him."

> Lombardi finally came in and said, "We are trying to get ready for the season. We have to have good practices. We were not having a good practice today. We can stay here as long as you want to, but we will have a good practice today. Everybody back out there."

We started the whole practice over.[34]

Pat Peppler assisted Coach Lombardi as director of player personnel and later went on to serve as head coach of the NFL's Atlanta Falcons. Peppler said, "Vince had been a teacher and coach at Saint Cecilia high school in New Jersey, so he was a strict man and knew all about hard work. He also knew a lot about psychology and how to get people to work harder than they thought they could. He was strict with his players, but he'd always pick a spot to let up when his players would least expect it."

Again and again, people who knew Vince Lombardi told me that he would take his players right to the brink of mutiny—then he'd stop and give them a moment for their souls to catch up with their bodies. Soon, he'd push them some more, always knowing exactly when to stop, when to inject a word of praise or encouragement. In short, Vince Lombardi had amazing *people skills*.

I would define people skills as a practical understanding of human emotions, motivations, and behavior, a deep empathy with other people, and the ability to adjust one's own behavior to produce positive results and healthy interactions. When people called Lombardi a "master psychologist," they were really saying that he was a master in the art of people skills.

LIKE DOGS—OR LIKE SONS?

Henry Jordan was a defensive tackle for the Green Bay Packers from 1959 to 1969 (he died of a heart attack in 1977 at the age of 42). Jordan famously said of his Green Bay coach, "Lombardi is very fair: he treats us all the same—like dogs." It's a clever line, and it has been quoted often. Most of Jordan's teammates agree that Lombardi was fair—but they bristle at the suggestion that Lombardi treated them "like dogs." In a January 1997 op-ed piece for the *New York Times*, Jerry Kramer spoke for many of his teammates when he observed that Jordan's quip was funny "but wildly inaccurate. Lombardi's genius was that he treated us all differently."[35]

Fairness should not be confused with sameness. If you have a five-year-old and a 15-year-old, and you give both children exactly the same treatment, the same allowance, the same bedtime, and the same privileges, then you are treating them the same, but you're not treating them fairly. Coach Lombardi was fair to his players because he did *not* treat them all the same. Royce Boyles told me, "As a leader, Vince Lombardi had the ability to treat each player individually. Henry Jordan's quote that Lombardi treated all the players like dogs just isn't true. Lombardi knew who he could kick in the tail and who needed to have his hair ruffled."

Sonny Jurgensen agreed. He dismissed the Jordan quote as untrue, adding, "Lombardi treated us like individuals and gave each of us what we individually needed in order to succeed. I think his background as a high school teacher helped make him a great head coach in the NFL." It's true. Vince Lombardi's experience as a teacher and coach at the high school and college levels undoubtedly sharpened his people skills for his role as a head coach in the NFL.

I don't think Henry Jordan himself believed his line about Lombardi treating his players all the same. It's a nifty one-liner, and Jordan couldn't resist the temptation of delivering it. But Jordan certainly must have realized how Coach Lombardi treated each of his players not only as an individual but also as a unique psychological puzzle to be solved. Lombardi studied the psyche of each of his players in an effort to find out how to best motivate that player. And Lombardi had Henry Jordan figured out. The proof is in a story Royce Boyles related to me, from the book he co-wrote with Dave Robinson, *The Lombardi Legacy*.

"Henry Jordan's widow, Olive, was a wonderful lady," Royce told me. "She passed away a few years ago. She told me a story that shows how inaccurate Henry's 'Lombardi-treated-us-all-alike' line was. One day, Olive was at the practice field, and she was noticeably pregnant. Lombardi walked up to her, patted her stomach, and smiled broadly. 'Good,' he said. Olive couldn't figure out why Lombardi was so pleased that she was going to have a baby, so she asked Henry about it. 'Lombardi loves it,' Henry told her, 'because that's another mouth to feed—and I'm going to have to work harder.'

"Vince Lombardi was a master motivator, and he knew how to get to that one lever inside every individual player that would fire him up. For one player it might be pride. For another, fear. Another, money. Another, religion. Lombardi could even reason with some guys. But for Henry Jordan, the key to motivation turned out to be Olive's pregnancy and another mouth to feed."

Andy Lukac played halfback from 1948 through 1950 under assistant coach Vince Lombardi at Fordham University. "After World War II," Andy told me, "Vince Lombardi, the offensive coordinator at Fordham, convinced me that I should play for him. He was consistent in his discipline and routine. He favored no one. You had to toe the line or you were not on the field. He respected any player who worked hard and was diligent in his effort. He didn't fool around with half-speed guys. Any practice was like a game, so I made sure I was consistent. If Vince Lombardi was consistent, I'd better be consistent, too.

"Lombardi was tough, but he tempered his toughness with fairness and even mercy at times. One year, we played a road game at Canisius College in Buffalo. We left from Grand Central Station, but our three quarterbacks missed the train. When we got to Buffalo, Coach Lombardi asked, 'Where are the quarterbacks?' We said, 'They missed the train, but they're catching the next train to Buffalo.'

"Well, Lombardi was furious. He was waiting for his quarterbacks to arrive for the team meeting, and he was really hot under the collar. When the quarterbacks arrived, they knew the trouble they were in. One of them, Billy White, said, 'Coach, we missed the train because I couldn't get my tie to tie the right way. You've always told us to look like gentlemen when we go out, and by the time I got my tie fixed, we had missed the train. I'm sorry, Coach.'

"Lombardi glared at them for a few seconds—and then he laughed. 'Get up to the room,' he said. 'We have a team meeting in fifteen minutes.'

"I had a chemistry class with a lab, which sometimes made me late to practice. One time, I arrived at the field late, and Coach

Lombardi threw me right into the scrimmage, even though I hadn't warmed up. I hit the quarterback and knocked him down, but in the process I pulled a hamstring. After practice, Coach Lombardi said, 'Andy, I'm very sorry. I didn't know you weren't warmed up. Go see the trainer, and he'll fix you up.' Coach Lombardi could be as tough as boot leather, but occasionally his merciful side came out—just when we needed it."

Coach Lombardi's greatest people skill was his ability to motivate his players. He used a combination of affirmation and fear—the carrot-and-stick approach—to get his players fired up to do what they really wanted to do. From his Jesuit training, Lombardi was undoubtedly familiar with the words Jesus said to His sleeping disciples in the Garden of Gethsemane: "The spirit is willing, but the flesh is weak."[36] Lombardi's Packers had the *spirit* to work hard, persevere, and win, but sometimes a player's *flesh* might need a kick in the pants. That kick is called *motivation*.

I knew Tom Brown even before he became a defensive back for the Green Bay Packers (I used to play baseball against him when I was a catcher for Wake Forest and he was an outfielder for the University of Maryland). His interception of a pass by Dallas Cowboys quarterback Don Meredith in the final seconds of the 1966 NFL Championship Game sent the Packers to Super Bowl I. Brown told me, "Coach Lombardi knew every play and assignment of each player. So you couldn't take a play off in practice or he'd call you on it. No player wanted to be embarrassed in front of his peers.

"He stressed to us that three plays make the difference in most football games, but you can only identify those three plays in hindsight. You never know in advance when those three pivotal plays are coming up. So you have to be ready on every play. You can't let up. Coach Lombardi kept us geared up for 100 percent effort on every play.

"Lombardi pushed us to bust through the wall of fatigue and keep going. Those endurance drills at the end of the practice were the real test. He'd have the film crew focus in on a player if Lombardi thought the guy was slacking off. That way, he'd have evidence. He was a great motivator, and he pushed us to be better. It was incredibly hard, but he made champions of us."

After Doug Hart was cut by the NFL St. Louis Cardinals, he retired from the game and went to work for Bell Helicopter Company. Coach Lombardi invited Hart to try out for the Packers. After Hart proved he still had it in an exhibition game against the Cowboys, Lombardi signed him to a contract. Hart went on to play eight seasons with the Green Bay Packers.

"After I played for Vince Lombardi," Hart told me, "I spent twenty years trying to figure out what set him apart. He said it best: 'When you have their hearts, you have their minds.' That means you draw people together in an emotional bond, so that they play as one and exert enormous willpower. As a result, players have a *reason* to play to the limit of their endurance when they face challenges and adversity. Emotion is a huge factor, especially when the chips are down. Emotion is the way you win when your back's against the wall. Emotion is the engine of motivation. Vince Lombardi was the best in the world at stirring the emotions of his players."

The late Dallas Cowboys head coach Tom Landry (who knew Lombardi well from their days together as assistant coaches with the New York Giants), once explained why *emotion* was such an important part of Lombardi's approach to coaching. "Lombardi's style of play was very different from ours," Landry said. "The Green Bay system of offense—we call it the basic system—was that you were going to run the power sweep regardless of what the other team put up against you. Run that play over and over until you can execute it in your sleep. It was all execution. So Lombardi had to develop the players to an emotional pitch, keep them doing their best all the time against a defense that knew what was coming. The Packers had to stay very high emotionally to win."[37]

One man with a unique vantage point on Coach Lombardi and his players was longtime NFL referee Jim Tunney. He told me, "Vince Lombardi was intense and focused because he wanted perfection on the field. He was a taskmaster, and he was tough on his players. But he had a heart of gold, and he was sensitive to all of them. He loved his players, and in spite of Lombardi's gruff demeanor and shouting, they felt it. They knew he cared about them. Lombardi had a father–son relationship with each of his players."

Willie Wood, who played safety for the Packers from 1960 to 1971, agrees: "Lombardi's secret was getting along with the players. He wasn't a dictator at all . . . Vince was a beautiful father-confessor, a man you could really confide in."[38]

In many different ways and different words, I heard Lombardi's old players express the same emotion: Vince Lombardi was hard on them. Sometimes he made them mad or hurt their feelings. But they knew he loved them, and they loved him like a father in return. Vince Lombardi didn't treat his players like dogs. He treated them like sons.

LOMBARDI'S GREATEST SKILL: MOTIVATION

Another message I heard again and again from Coach Lombardi's players was how much they wanted to please him. Some players feared Lombardi, some loved Lombardi, but all wanted to make him proud.

Offensive tackle Steve Wright told me, "Coach Lombardi projected such an aura of leadership and authority that you wanted to please him every day. The real mission was to do everything exactly the way he told you. If you did, you'd be successful. I was drafted by the Packers on the fifth round out of Alabama as a defensive end. I was overwhelmed in training camp, so Coach Lombardi said, 'Put him in the offensive line.' I blew everyone out, and that's how I became an offensive tackle.

"One game in Chicago, I banged the outside of my knee and couldn't get back on my feet for a few moments. Then I saw Coach Lombardi coming out on the field to check on me. I instantly felt panic. My first thought was, 'I'm okay. I've *got* to be okay.' I didn't want to disappoint the man."

Pat Richter was a wide receiver and punter for the Washington Redskins from 1963 to 1970. He told me, "Coach Lombardi would push you and demand things of you until you were ready to rebel. Then he'd find a way to lift you up and make you feel so good about yourself. One day in practice, I got my nose busted doing blocking drills. I took two more blocks before they took me into the hospital to get my nose packed with gauze. I showed up the next day at practice and jogged a little. I hadn't gone far before I heard Coach Lombardi's voice—'Get over here, Richter. You take it easy today.' I later heard from a teammate that Lombardi said about me, 'The kid showed a lot of guts.' It was an incredible feeling, hearing those words. He was a tough coach, but you'd do anything to please the man."

Vince Lombardi wasn't one to shower compliments like confetti. Instead, he doled out compliments sparingly and saved them for strategic moments, when they would do the most good and have the greatest impact. Wide receiver Gary Knafelc played nine seasons with the Packers, both before and during the Lombardi Era. "I can still hear Vince Lombardi's voice in my head to this day," Gary told me. "One day, during training camp at Saint Norbert's, we had a big scrimmage. That night, Bart Starr and I had dinner together.

"Afterward, we were walking down the street when we saw Vince Lombardi. We crossed the street to avoid him. He crossed the street, too. I thought, *Oh, no. This is it. Lombardi's gonna cut me from the team.* Lombardi approached us and said, 'Gary, you had some great blocks today.' That's all he said, then he walked on by. He made me feel like King Kong. After that I felt that I could do anything out on the field."

Wide receiver Boyd Dowler played 11 seasons with the Green Bay Packers and one with the Washington Redskins. He told me, "If Vince Lombardi got on you, you deserved it. You always knew what to expect from Coach Lombardi because he was so consistent. He motivated all of us, year after year. If you'd buy in and do what he taught you, then you'd be just fine. But if you lost your focus or did anything stupid, you wouldn't be around. So you always wanted to please Coach Lombardi. You didn't want him mad at you, but more than that, you didn't want him to be disappointed in you.

"His greatest skill was motivation. He would use anything and everything to get us fired up, to get us to believe in ourselves. He talked about a lot more than football. He often quoted Scripture to us, talked about the importance of family and good character, and he told us the lessons we were learning on the football field were lessons about life. He believed in us and made us believe in ourselves. He motivated us to do things we didn't think we could do. Coach Lombardi was incredibly inspirational."

Hall of Fame running back Paul Hornung told me, "Vince Lombardi motivated all of us so that we were always on the same page. He made sure of that. Winning was always his focus. Lombardi taught us how to play together as a unit, every man carrying out his assignment as part of the greater whole. He taught us how to win, and that it takes more than talent. You have to be sharp mentally and know exactly what you're doing out there on the field. Coach Lombardi always had us ready to play. We had a job to do and all of us knew what we had to do to be successful. We didn't want to let him down."

Vince Lombardi tried to get to know each man—what got each player fired up, where each player's breaking point was, when to push harder, when to ease off—but sometimes he got it wrong. Wide receiver Bob Long earned championship rings in Super Bowls I and II. He told me, "Lombardi handled each guy differently. One day at practice, he was screaming at some guys and not at others—and I was one of the guys he was yelling at. So I went over to him, took him aside, and said, 'Coach, I'm a self-motivator. You don't have to yell at me. Just tell me what you want me to do, and I'll do it.'

"And you know what? He never yelled at me again. Some guys needed that, but I didn't. Coach Lombardi knew how to motivate each of us in the way that worked best. If he could get you to work hard, keep your mental focus, carry out your assignments, and do it all with a positive attitude, he was pleased. More than anything else, he wanted us to go out there with a positive attitude. He wanted us to think like winners."

Lombardi's secretary, Lori Keck, had enormous admiration for her boss. But there was one time when Vince Lombardi almost pushed the boss-secretary relationship to the breaking point. She told me, "One time, Lombardi was going on vacation to the Caribbean. Before he left, he called the girls into his office and gave us all some instructions. Then he said, 'Now, while I'm gone, I don't want any sloughing off.' And I just bristled! When I get angry, nobody has to guess. *They know.* I didn't say anything, but Lombardi knew.

"He looked at me and said, 'Lorraine?' (He never called me Lori, always Lorraine.) I said, 'Well, who has?' He said, 'I'm just saying.' And he left the office to begin his vacation.

"The next day, he called and said, 'Are you still mad at me?' I said, 'Well!' He said, 'The reason I said that with you there was because I knew you'd be able to take it. I know you don't slough off. I was trying to make an impression on some other people. But I knew I could use you as an example.' It didn't turn out quite the way he wanted, but I accepted his apology and things were fine after that.

"I later found out that Lombardi often used that same approach with his players. He'd pick on his best player just to show that he didn't play favorites. You can't treat your second-stringers that way, but if you treat your top player that way, you can make an impression on everyone else. But it's risky. You have to make sure you only do it to someone you know can handle it."

USING PEOPLE SKILLS TO IMPOSE DISCIPLINE

Coach and commentator John Madden was heavily influenced by Vince Lombardi's coaching style and philosophy. Madden was an assistant coach at Allan Hancock College in Santa Maria when Simon & Schuster published Lombardi's book (written with W. C. Heinz), *Run to Daylight!: Vince Lombardi's Diary of One Week with the Green Bay Packers.* Madden bought the book, devoured it, studied it, and lived in it. When the book was reissued in 2014, the publisher asked Madden to write a new foreword for the book. Madden was honored.

He wrote about the lessons that he learned from Coach Lombardi's book. "In reading how Vince Lombardi dealt with his players," Madden said, "I learned that nothing can be phony . . . You can copy another coach's philosophy, but you can't copy his personality. That's where some young coaches get in trouble. They think, well, this guy is a great coach, I want to be like him. They try to shape their personality like his. But you can't be somebody else. You've got to be who you are."

Another lesson John Madden learned from Coach Lombardi: "As a coach, you always have to act the opposite of how your team is doing." In other words, if your players are on a winning streak, and the fans and sports writers are inflating their egos, your job as coach is to bring them down to earth. On the other hand, if your players are on a losing streak, if they are getting slammed by the fans and hammered by the sports writers, then your job is to lift them up and get them to believe in themselves.

Madden says that Lombardi's book even helped his marriage. He recalled, "When my wife Virginia read *Run To Daylight!*, it helped her to understand me. Vince Lombardi would get up in the morning and start arguing with his wife Marie to get himself in the mood to yell at his players. I did that with Virginia, too. I probably did it naturally, but Virginia came to understand *why* I was doing it."

John Madden said he also learned how to discipline players from reading Lombardi's book: "When you chew out your players, you shouldn't pick on a second-stringer. Hey, a second-stringer is always more vulnerable because he's more likely to make mistakes. That's why he's a second-stringer." Singling out a second-stringer makes it look like you're bullying a weaker player. If you must chew somebody out, Madden advises, "chew out your best players." And make sure they know that this is discipline, not a personal attack.

Madden learned from Lombardi to always tell his players, "I respect you, I love you, but when you make a mistake, we've got to go over it." This approach made it easier for both Lombardi and Madden to discipline their players without building up resentment or damaging the player–coach relationship.[39]

Lombardi biographer David Maraniss told me, "There was a fine line between love and hate with Lombardi and his players. He pushed his players on a daily basis, and that's where the hate developed. But over the long haul, they loved him. Vince Lombardi knew when to pull back because he was a master psychologist and he knew what buttons to push with each guy.

"For example, Paul Hornung could take anything Lombardi dished out. Lombardi would absolutely blister Hornung and even fine him. Hornung would accept it. A lot of other players couldn't take it—Bart Starr, for example. Starr would have recoiled at that kind of treatment. So Lombardi would pour out his wrath on Paul Hornung—and it worked. When Lombardi unleashed on Hornung, the entire team shaped up."

There's a fascinating legend about Coach Lombardi that has been widely circulated over the years. As the story goes, it was 1964 and Packers all-pro center Jim Ringo's contract was up for renewal. Ringo showed up at Coach Lombardi's office with an agent. "I don't negotiate with agents," Lombardi allegedly said. "Hold on, let me make a phone call." Lombardi left the office for five minutes, then returned and told Ringo and his agent, "Like I said, I don't negotiate with agents. Jim, you've just been traded to Philadelphia."

Now, Jim Ringo was one of Lombardi's best players, and he anchored the Packers Sweep. So the notion that Coach Lombardi would deal Jim Ringo to another team with just a five-minute phone call is rather shocking. And, to be clear, the story is *not* true. It never happened. What is the truth behind the legend?

Well, Jim Ringo *was* traded to Philadelphia—but the trade wasn't negotiated in a five-minute phone call. Believe me, that's not how things are done in professional sports. Ringo and his agent didn't negotiate directly with Vince Lombardi, either. They dealt with Pat Peppler, the Packers' director of player personnel. And Ringo wasn't shipped out of Green Bay against his will. He would have gladly stayed in Green Bay for more money, but he also wanted to play for Philadelphia, near his hometown of Phillipsburg, New Jersey. The trade sent Ringo and fullback Earl Gros to the Philadelphia Eagles in exchange for linebacker Lee Roy Caffey and a first-round draft choice.

So, if the five-minute trade never happened, where did the legend come from? It came from Lombardi himself! He told that story many times, saying, "Ringo and his agent got out of my office in a hurry! And if any other player comes to me with an ultimatum, he'll get traded just as fast!" Lombardi used that story to keep his players from making huge salary demands. Lombardi wanted his players to believe that if he was this quick to trade his star center, then he'd trade anybody, anytime. The legend of Jim Ringo and the five-minute trade gave Lombardi a little extra leverage at contract time—and probably on the practice field as well.[40]

I'm not suggesting leaders should spread untrue stories in order to gain an advantage. I'm saying that, as leaders, we need to be willing to use our top-performing people as examples. All too often, leaders allow themselves to be intimidated by the stars on their team, and these stars become undisciplined and uncoachable. Once you are no longer able to discipline your star players, discipline starts breaking down across the board. If your players suspect you play favorites and treat some of them unfairly, there will be bitterness, selfishness, and mutiny in the ranks. But if your players see you as tough but fair, you'll maintain your authority.

Packers wide receiver Carroll Dale found that Coach Lombardi could be reasonable and fair at contract-negotiating time. A committed Christian and the team chapel leader, he asked Coach Lombardi for an unusual concession in his contract. "Coach," Dale said, "I tithe ten percent of my salary to my church in Virginia. If you'll send my church ten percent of my salary, I'll sign." Lombardi saw it as a "yes–yes" deal and quickly agreed. This way, one-tenth of Dale's pay didn't show up on the ledger as gross salary but was paid directly from the Packers to the church as a tax-deductible donation.[41]

Former Packers defensive back Dale Hackbart recalled, "Vince Lombardi was a disciplinarian and his players knew that. He treated us all fairly and didn't let us get away with much. He kept everyone in check. For example, he was a stickler about promptness. He'd say, 'If you're ten minutes early, that means you're five minutes late.' So if the bus to the airport was to leave at noon, you'd better be on that bus at 11:45 because Coach Lombardi was staring at his watch and counting down. He'd leave people. He was a time-checker."

Wide receiver Red Mack told me, "In 1966, I got picked up by the Packers from Atlanta. When I got to Green Bay, the first place I went to was Vince Lombardi's office. He welcomed me to the Packers organization and from that point on I realized that he treated all of us as equal teammates. I was no different than Bart Starr in Lombardi's mind. We all had a job to do. I did my job and got to play in Super Bowl I."

Sometimes, Lombardi's disciplinary approach came as a complete surprise. Lee Folkins made this discovery after he was drafted by the Packers in 1961. Folkins played tight end as a backup to Ron Kramer.

He was part of the Packers 1961 NFL Championship team but was traded the following season to the Dallas Cowboys. "I only played one season for Coach Lombardi," he told me, "but in that season, he had as much impact on my life as my father. Who knows what kind of career I might have had if I had stayed in Green Bay? Lombardi had a way of getting the best out of everyone. He could make an average player great and a great player legendary.

"As a football strategist, he believed in keeping it simple. He often said it didn't matter if the opponent knew what play we were going to run. We were going to prevail simply because of our stronger will to win. He called it 'Spartanism.'

"I'll tell you a story about Coach Lombardi—but I'm not proud of this incident. I was a rookie player on Lombardi's first NFL championship team in 1961. In those days, the NFL champion would play the College All-Stars in the next year's pre-season opener. The game was played at Soldier Field in Chicago, August 3, 1962.

"During the third quarter, one of the college all-stars, Hank Rivera from Oregon, hit me with what I thought was a cheap shot. I lost my temper and went after Rivera—but a referee stepped between us to break up the fight. The punch I aimed it Rivera hit the ref instead, and the poor guy went down on the grass, out cold.

"I was ejected from the game—the first and only time in my athletic career it ever happened. I sat on the bench for the rest of the game—ashamed, embarrassed, and dreading what Coach Lombardi was going to do to me. The whole time I sat there, Coach did not approach me—and I certainly wasn't about to approach him. We won, 42 to 20—but I didn't feel like celebrating. We headed back into the locker room, and I avoided the reporters and Coach Lombardi— but I knew I'd have to face him eventually.

"I was the last to leave the locker room, and as I boarded the bus, Coach Lombardi and his wife Marie sat in their customary place up front. As I walked up the steps of the bus, I paused and apologized to Lombardi for my actions on the field. I told him that hitting the referee was an accident, but there was no excuse for my behavior. Then I waited for the yelling to begin.

"Lombardi's reaction was the last thing in the world I expected. He broke out in his loud laugh, slapped me on the shoulder, and said, 'Don't worry about it, Lee. Anytime you hit a referee, it's okay with me.'

"Now, I don't want anyone to misunderstand his meaning. Lombardi was kidding, and he only joked like that because he knew I'd *never* think it was okay to hit an official. But I think the whole time I had been avoiding him during the game, he'd been watching me out of the corner of his eye. He knew I was suffering and punishing myself more harshly than anything he could do to me.

"Vince Lombardi had more understanding of what makes people tick than anyone else I've ever known. He knew when to lower the boom and when to laugh it off. He knew exactly what each player needed at any given time. We all feared him, but we respected him and loved him. He continues to influence my life to this day."

LEADERS DEAL WITH PEOPLE FACE-TO-FACE

One people skill that gets too little attention as a leadership trait is the willingness to deal face-to-face with unpleasant personnel tasks. That's one of the defining differences between a boss and a leader. Any boss can delegate distasteful chores to underlings—and that's why bosses always leave bitter feelings and resentment in their wake.

But a genuine leader shoulders personal responsibility for unpleasant tasks, earning respect and appreciation in the process.

Red Mack told me, "In 1967, Coach Lombardi decided to release me from the Packers, but he didn't send one of his assistants to give me the bad news. He called me into his office and told me his decision, face-to-face. I could tell it wasn't easy for him. Nobody enjoys giving bad news. But Coach Lombardi had a way of looking you in the eye and making you feel better about it. He gave it to me straight, and he did it himself. I've always appreciated that."

Phil Vandersea was a Packers linebacker and defensive end for four seasons, 1965 through 1969. He told me, "To Coach Lombardi, the team was always the most important thing—not the individual. He could be tough, even harsh sometimes, yet we always knew it was because he cared about the team. If the team succeeds, we all succeed.

"Vince Lombardi had a good heart, and even though the team came first, he cared for each of his players in a personal way. In 1967, when New Orleans came into the NFL as an expansion team, the Saints selected me as one of their expansion draft picks. Coach Lombardi called me personally and gave me the news straight from the shoulder. Then he said, 'Phil, we didn't want to lose you. Good luck to you.' I appreciated that. He showed compassion to his guys. He was honest and direct, and that's what you want in a coach."

Leadership entails a responsibility to look your people in the eye and give them the bad news yourself. The willingness to deal honestly, directly, and personally with your people is a people skill that will always serve you well in your leadership role.

HE COULD TEAR YOU DOWN AND BUILD YOU UP

Another people skill we don't hear enough of these days is the skill of edifying other people. Edifying comes from the same root word as *edifice*, meaning a building. To edify someone is to *build* that person up, to make that person stronger. We can build people up morally, intellectually, emotionally, and spiritually through instruction and encouragement. Lombardi's players frequently told me he was always finding ways to build up his players, to edify his team.

Linebacker Dave Robinson told me, "When the team was down, he'd build us up. One time, when we failed to score in the closing minutes of the game, Lombardi told us, 'We didn't lose, we just ran out of time.' But after big wins, we'd be all excited and flying high, and Coach Lombardi would bring us down to earth. He knew that if we celebrated all week and listened to the adulation from the fans and read our press clipping, telling us how great we are, we were asking for trouble. Our opponent would be primed for us, ready to play the game of their lives. Lombardi knew he had to keep us on an even keel—never too low, never too high."

Wide receiver Carroll Dale told me, "Vince Lombardi was a very emotional coach, yet he was able to set his emotions aside when he came to dealing with his players. When the Packers won, he'd chew on us for the mistakes we've made. He made sure we didn't get overconfident. Overconfidence was the biggest threat to success. When we lost, he wouldn't pile on and make us feel worse. He knew how badly his players felt after a loss, especially the players of character. So even though we had made mistakes, he'd focus on how we would improve for the next game.

"Coaches will often yank a player out of the game for one mistake. Not Lombardi. If an end dropped a pass, he'd stay with that guy and help him regain his confidence. If you are the best player for the job, you play.

"If everything a leader does is for the good of the organization, people will follow that leader. People will accept almost anything from that leader if they believe it will lead to success. Lombardi was demanding, but he made us winners, so we wanted to meet his demands. When he criticized the players' performance, there was only one response: 'Yes, sir.' That meant you heard what he said. Any other response was making excuses.

"Vince Lombardi stressed that every player had an important job to accomplish, the only job that mattered—winning. And after you win, you don't slack off, you don't rest. The more success you have, the better you have to be the next time. You have to be a much better team in order to repeat your success. And we were."

Packers quarterback Zeke Bratkowski was called Bart Starr's "super sub" because he was a backup quarterback with starter-level skills (he went on to a long career as a coach in the NFL and was an early advocate of aerobic training for football players). Zeke told me, "We never knew what Coach Lombardi would say. After a loss, when we were waiting for him to land in the middle of us, he'd be more gentle toward us than after a win. Sometimes he'd yell and get all over you during practice, then afterwards he'd come by your locker and cheer you up. At training camp, he once said to me, 'Is your family here?' I said, 'No.' He said, 'Well, get them here right away.' He was a big believer in the importance of family, and he taught that family helps keep a player centered and focused. That was also Lombardi's way of letting me know I'd made the roster."

And five-time All-Pro guard Jerry Kramer remembers Coach Lombardi as "a very, very sensitive man. He could tear you apart, but he also had the knack of saying or doing just the right thing to bring you back up and make you believe you could be a lot better than you really were."[42]

Kramer shared with me an incident to illustrate how Coach Lombardi used his considerable people skills to prevent his players from getting swelled heads. He and fellow guard Fuzzy Thurston were the two anchors of Coach Lombardi's near-unstoppable Packers Sweep running attack. "One year," Kramer told me, "Fuzzy Thurston and I got a big write-up in the *Chicago Tribune*, saying we were the best guards in the NFL. Well, Coach Lombardi knew he didn't dare let Fuzzy and me start believing our press clippings. So he waited for just the right moment to jump all over that one. One day in practice, Fuzzy and I messed up a play pretty badly. And off he went, sounding almost gleeful! 'Best guards in the NFL! Hah! We've got the *worst* guards in the NFL!' Then he turned and walked away.

"Well, I was boiling mad! I took off after him and walked right behind him, ready to explode. I was honestly ready to punch him, and I didn't care what happened to me. I might be kicked out of football, but that didn't matter. Lombardi was pacing around, looking at his shoes, and I shadowed him with my fists clenched. He knew I was there, but he wouldn't look at me. I couldn't catch his eye.

"The next practice play, I just walked up to the line of scrimmage—and I was so mad, I didn't run the play. I was out of control. All I needed was to catch his eye, just one look from him, and I was going after him. But he wouldn't give me the satisfaction.

"Finally, I went over to the sidelines, and I began to simmer down. I was still mad, sort of pouting, but I had started coming to my senses. Lombardi knew me well, and he could read me. He could tell when it was safe to talk to me, so he came over to me and slapped me on the shoulder pads and tousled my hair. He said, 'Jerry, I wasn't talking about you! Come on, now!'

"That was Coach. Yes, he could push you right to the edge, where you were ready to explode. But then he'd re-establish communication and get things straightened out before the practice ended. He'd never let a problem sit and fester. He wanted to get problems out of the way in order to keep the lines of communication open. But he also made sure that we didn't get too full of ourselves.

"Coach Lombardi was a great judge of talent. He knew what we were capable of achieving even more than we did. He knew whether a player was maxing out his talent or just coasting and collecting a paycheck. Vince Lombardi wanted everything you had. He was determined to get the maximum effort out of everybody, from his superstars to the guys who were hanging on to the bottom of the roster by their fingernails.

"He would do whatever it takes—build you up, tear you down, teasing it out of you, threaten it out of you, make you laugh, make you mad, intimidate you, motivate you. Whatever it took to get guys to play to the extreme limits of their ability, Vince Lombardi would do it."

In *Run to Win*, Donald T. Phillips wrote about Coach Lombardi's unique approach to applying people skills to the task of motivating people performance:

> Learning about the intricacies of the people on his team was, for Lombardi, an ongoing process—as important to him as the subtle details of the game of football . . . When he realized that harsh methods didn't work with a player, he'd quickly change his approach—as he did, for instance, with left linebacker Dan Currie.
>
> "Where criticism just bounces off Ray Nitschke, it cut so deep into Currie that I have to be careful," noted

Lombardi. "My first year here I chewed him out in front of the others just once and I knew immediately that he resented it and that it wouldn't help. Even in private you have to be careful how you handle him, but if you tell him he's playing well he'll go out there and kill himself for you."

Wide receiver Max McGee told Phillips that, once he had earned Coach Lombardi's respect, he never had to take part in the Packers' infamous "nutcracker drill." McGee took Lombardi aside and said, "Coach, I can sweep-block for you, but it will not do me any good to have Ray Nitschke hit me with a forearm."

Coach Lombardi didn't want his players to think he was showing favoritism to McGee. So he quietly gave McGee a way to get around the nutcracker drill. "You just get in line for that drill," Lombardi told McGee, "and when you get near the front of the line, just step out and sneak back to the end."

"I did that for nine years," McGee told Phillips. "I never once did the nutcracker drill." Through gestures like that, Coach Lombardi won the love of his players—and their loyalty translated to extra effort on the field. "He can get that extra ten percent out of an individual," McGee concluded. "Multiply ten percent times forty men on a team times fourteen games a season—and you're going to win."[43]

DEALING WITH THE MEDIA

Many people, when they hear the term *people skills*, think of a special capacity to be charming, gentle, and sympathetic. Well, none of those adjectives describes Vince Lombardi's interactions with his players on the practice field—though he was often understanding and empathetic when a player needed a personal word of encouragement. Lombardi often treated people in the media the same way he treated his players—with swearing and verbal abuse.

Bob Schulze was the sports director at Green Bay's WFRV-TV during the Lombardi Era. Prior to his first encounter with Coach Lombardi, Schulze had interviewed high school and college football coaches and always found them to be media friendly. Meeting Coach Lombardi was like a punch in the face. When Schulze and his camera crew came to practices, Lombardi would heap as much verbal abuse on them as he would on his players. He'd yell at them for setting up their cameras too close to the field, or for getting in his way, or for asking "stupid" questions.

"What really got Lombardi's cork," Schulze told me, "was reporters asking him questions when he thought we already knew the answers. He couldn't understand that our viewers wanted to hear the answers from his lips, not ours."

Now, I know what you're thinking. You're wondering how a story about Coach Lombardi screaming and cussing at sports reporters is a story about people skills. Stay with me. All will become clear.

Shulze told me that, after his abrasive encounters with Coach Lombardi, he would go home and rant to his wife, Mary Lou, about what a miserable, raving tyrant Lombardi was. Naturally, Mary Lou developed a mental image of Vince Lombardi as one of the most unpleasant human beings who ever lived.

At the end of the 1962 football season, Coach Lombardi invited members of the sports media and their spouses to his home for a cocktail party. Bob and Mary Lou arrived at the Lombardi home and were ushered downstairs to a large family room, with a wet bar and a wall lined with Lombardi's prized collection of wind-up toys. Lombardi stood at the foot of the steps, smiling broadly, arms outstretched.

In those moments, Bob Shulze saw something in Vince Lombardi he had never seen at the practice field: *charm.* Bucketloads of it. Lombardi gushed, "You must be Bob's beautiful wife, Mary Lou! How does a guy like him deserve a girl like you?"

Then Lombardi guided Mary Lou over to the bar, proudly showed her his collection of wind-up toys, and showed her how they worked. He was a sparkling conversationalist, a genial host, and he dazzled Mary Lou. Later, as the Schulzes were leaving, Mary Lou seemed to float up the stairs on a cloud—and she asked Bob, "Why did you say all those nasty things about that nice, sweet man?"

Bob Schulze had to admire Coach Lombardi's people skills. In his interactions with reporters—and their wives—he always knew exactly what he was doing. He would use verbal invective and intimidation when it served his purpose—but he could also turn on the charm.

Bob Schulze and Vince Lombardi continued to have a stormy relationship throughout Lombardi's tenure in Green Bay. Schulze often daydreamed of telling Lombardi off. His opportunity finally came in early 1969, when Lombardi announced his departure from Green Bay. Schulze was invited to a farewell party for the coach—and he was surprised to discover that he was actually going to *miss* the old so-and-so. He took a copy of Lombardi's *Run to Daylight* to the event to get it autographed.

When Schulze had a chance to talk to Lombardi for a few minutes, he actually became misty-eyed and a little choked up. Lombardi inscribed a note in the book and handed it back to Schulze—but Schulze didn't read the inscription until he got back to his car. Lombardi had written:

To Bob Schulze,
a prince in his field,
from Vince Lombardi,
a pauper in his.

Schulze was amazed at the warmth and generosity of those words. That was the last time he ever saw Coach Lombardi. In the spring of 1970, Bob Schulze's basement flooded, and his autographed copy of *Run to Daylight* was destroyed. In September 1970, Vince Lombardi died of cancer in Washington, D.C.

FUN IS A PEOPLE SKILL

One people skill that deserves more attention as a leadership trait is the ability to create an atmosphere of fun. A leader should be enthusiastic and excited, and should enjoy the leadership role. When the leader is having fun in the leadership role, followers will have fun being part of the team. Fun is an essential component of morale, and strong morale is essential to a team's peak performance.

Vince Lombardi enjoyed his role. He had fun as a football coach at every level, from high school to college to the NFL. Colonel Karl Otto Kuckhahn was one of the last surviving members of the Lombardi-era West Point teams. I spoke to Kuckhahn in September 2013, just a few weeks before his death at age 87. He played fullback at Army in the late 1940s. He remembered assistant coach Vince Lombardi as a man who always had fun on the football field.

"On the team, we called Coach Lombardi 'Grumpy' for the same reason you call a bald guy 'Curly.' Vince Lombardi was always grinning, always laughing, always having a great time. Sure, he'd yell, he'd get in your face, and he was really passionate about the game.

But he was never gloomy or grumpy, so naturally we nicknamed him 'Grumpy.' He liked the nickname, though the other coaches could never understand why we called him that.

"At first, Coach Lombardi called me by my first name, Karl. But during the games, he heard the cadet corps chanting my middle name from the stands—'Otto! Otto!' From then on, Lombardi always called me Otto.

"Coach Lombardi was always excited and energetic, and his excitement was contagious. We all caught it. Vince Lombardi was a good coach, a good fellow, and we all admired him. He praised us a lot. But we had to work hard for him every day, because he'd make us practice and practice a play until we got it right."

I heard a similar assessment of Coach Lombardi's personality from Tom Brown, a defensive back with the Green Bay Packers. "Vince Lombardi believed you need three things to be an effective leader," Brown told me. "First, you must have control of the team. You need to be an authority figure. Second, you must have intelligence—the ability to perceive the situation clearly, to think things through, and to make good decisions. Third—and this one surprises people—Coach Lombardi believed you need to have fun. You have to be enthusiastic about your leadership role. You must love your work. And you have to be able to laugh at yourself. Coach Lombardi had all of those qualities, and he proved he was able to laugh at himself, especially when he'd get into it with Max McGee."

Though Coach Lombardi could be harsh and demanding toward his players, he was genial and gracious in his interactions with the public and the media. Dave Anderson, longtime *New York Times* columnist, told me, "I was writing for the *New York Journal American* in the 1950s when Vince Lombardi and Tom Landry were assistant coaches under Lee Howell. After each home game, I would do a sidebar and diagram of the big play of the game. I went to Coach Howell and asked him for help in drawing up the play. He said, 'Talk to Vince.' That's how I got to know Vince Lombardi.

"If you were a friend from Vince Lombardi's New York days, he would treat you like royalty for life. He was always very kind to me. Later, when he moved to Green Bay and to Washington, he was still the same guy and always very kind to me. Whether in Green Bay or anywhere else, in his heart, Lombardi was a New Yorker forever."

I also interviewed Art McNally, the former director of officiating for the NFL. He recalls, "In 1965, Green Bay and San Francisco played the last game of the season with the division title at stake. Late in the first half, 49ers quarterback John Brodie pitched out to John David Crow. The ball ended up on the ground, and the Packers' Willie Wood scooped it up and ran it in for a touchdown. As the Packers lined up for the extra point, referee Chuck Heborling came to me and said, 'That was a pitch out and Crow never had possession of the ball.' Well, that voided the touchdown.

"So I went into the Green Bay huddle and said, 'Captain Starr, that was not a touchdown,' and I explained why. For a moment, nobody said a word. Then Bart Starr said to me, 'You go tell the man.' So I went over to the sideline to inform Lombardi. As you can imagine—and to put it mildly—Lombardi was not happy.

"The game ended up in a tie, which forced a showdown with Baltimore. The Packers won in overtime. Twenty-five years later, I happened to see John David Crow at an event and we talked about that game. He told me we called it right—he never had possession of the ball."

"One time, after I was named NFL's supervisor of officials, I was in the New York NFL headquarters during the off-season. I bumped into Vince Lombardi, and this was just three years after our call had taken a touchdown away from him and nearly cost him the game. Some coaches can hold a grudge forever. Not Lombardi. He congratulated me on my appointment, and he said, 'We just lost a good referee.' That was one of the nicest things anyone ever said to me."

The ability to have fun and spread a feeling of excitement and enthusiasm wherever you go is a people skill—and a leadership skill. Great leaders like Vince Lombardi are fun to be around.

THE TURNAROUND OF RAY NITSCHKE

Middle linebacker Ray Nitschke anchored one of the best defensive squads in NFL history. I wish I could have interviewed him for this book, but in 1998, Nitschke died at age 61 of a heart attack. The stories he could have told!

Vince Lombardi had an enormous impact on the life of Ray Nitschke. Coming from the mean streets of Chicago, Nitschke needed a firm hand from a tough-guy coach like Lombardi. His father died when he was three, and his mother died when he was 13. Raised by his older brothers, he grew up about the way you'd expect a boy without parents to grow up. His saving grace was that he excelled in sports and received a football scholarship to the University of Illinois.

In 1956, in a game against Ohio State, Nitschke was playing without a face mask. An Ohio State guard elbowed him in the mouth, and four front teeth went flying. Nitschke went to the sideline, shoved a wad of cotton gauze into his mouth, went back onto the field, and played the rest of the game spitting blood onto the grass (just as a young Vince Lombardi had done in a 1936 Fordham game against the University of Pittsburgh).

Nitschke wanted to play professional football for his hometown Chicago Bears but was drafted by the Packers in 1958. Nitschke had to get a roadmap to find Green Bay, Wisconsin. He sat out most of his first season, when the Packers were coached by "Scooter" McLean. The following year, Green Bay hired Vince Lombardi as head coach and general manager—and Ray Nitschke's life began to change.

When Lombardi arrived in Green Bay, he had questions about Nitschke—a loud, angry, unruly two-fisted drinker who rebelled against team discipline. Nitschke's biographer, Edward Gruver, wrote:

> Privately the Packer coaching staff worried that Nitschke's wild ways might end in tragedy. Lombardi confided to friends that he thought Nitschke "might kill somebody" and threatened to trade his troubled middle linebacker in 1960.
>
> "Raymond was headed for bad trouble," halfback Paul Hornung remembered. "His drinking was out of control."[44]

During his first season as head coach of the Packers, Lombardi was slow to give Nitschke any playing time. Frustrated, Nitschke tried to get more playing time by being a burr under Lombardi's saddle. Seated on the bench, Nitschke would wait until Lombardi walked by, and then he would shout, "Just call me the judge, 'cause I'm always on the bench."

Lombardi's reply: "Hey, Nitschke."

"Yeah?"

"Shaddup."[45]

Over time, however, the Lombardi–Nitschke relationship began to thaw, and Ray Nitschke saw more playing time. The more Nitschke played, the better he got. The better he got, the more playing time Lombardi gave him.

Around that time, Nitschke became smitten with a waitress at a local restaurant. Her name was Jackie Forchette, a devout Catholic farm girl from Michigan. Jackie was well aware of Ray Nitschke's reputation as a drinker and a brawler, and she wanted nothing to do with him. One night, she was on a dinner date with a man when Ray Nitschke strode in, walked up to their table, and said to Jackie's date, "Why don't you tell Jackie about your wife and kids?"

It was true, the man was married—but he had told Jackie he was single. Ray had done a little detective work.

"Beat it," Nitschke said. The man left the restaurant—and Nitschke sat down and had dinner with Jackie. That was the beginning of their courtship.

It was a rocky courtship at first. Jackie disapproved of his drinking, but he didn't want to give it up. Then, one night when he was out driving with Jackie, they had a bad accident and rolled the car. Ray and Jackie both walked away from the accident, but it frightened Ray Nitschke to realize how close he had come to killing the woman he loved. He gave up drinking, and (except for one brief and unfortunate relapse) he never touched another drop.

Ray and Jackie were married in June 1961. They later adopted three children, and Ray became an exemplary role model for his sons John and Richard and his daughter Amy. The two most important adults in Nitschke's life, Jackie and Coach Lombardi, had a steadying and stabilizing influence on him—and so did fatherhood. Nitschke later said, "Having a family really solidified my life. Before I got married I was kind of runnin' them streets."[46]

Nitschke's Green Bay teammates were amazed at the change in him. "It was the greatest thing I've ever seen," said Paul Hornung. "He adopted three kids, became a model citizen, and just did a fantastic job turning his life around."[47]

Deprived of a childhood of his own, Ray Nitschke was able to experience a healthy, happy childhood through his own three kids. And in many ways, Coach Lombardi became the father-figure Nitschke had missed ever since he was three years old. Nitschke's daughter Amy credited both Jackie and Vince Lombardi for turning her father's life around. Jackie and Lombardi, Amy said, "were the two people my dad looked to at the time for any kind of guidance and strength."[48] Coach Lombardi's people skills played a big role not just in Ray Nitschke's football career but in his life as a husband and father as well.

Not only did Nitschke stop drinking and carousing, but he even cleaned up his language. Bill Curry, who retired from coaching in 2012, joined the Packers as a rookie center from Georgia Tech in 1965. Ray Nitschke took a fatherly interest in Curry. During a game against the Chicago Bears, Nitschke told Curry, "If you make a play over by the Bears' bench, just hurry back to the huddle."

"Why is that?" Curry asked.

"There's a short, fat coach on the Bears' bench," Nitschke said. "He's got a real loud mouth and you shouldn't hear that kind of stuff. I don't want you exposed to that kind of filth."

Just a few years earlier, Nitschke himself had been a fountain of "that kind of filth." The transformation in his character was nothing short of miraculous. But the fact that Ray Nitschke had stopped drinking, brawling, and cussing didn't mean he had gone soft. On the field, he was more physically intimidating than ever. At times, he even seemed to be invulnerable.

On one occasion, when the Packers were working out during a windstorm, a gust of wind blew over a 15-foot iron tower. The falling tower knocked Ray Nitschke to the ground.

Lombardi shouted, "Who got hit?"

Bart Starr had witnessed the accident. "Nitschke!" he called back.

Lombardi shrugged, turned to his team, and called for the next workout. He didn't even check to see if Nitschke was okay. Lombardi assumed that Nitschke was indestructible, and it was a fairly valid assumption.

Nitschke got up and examined his helmet. One of the bolts on the tower had punched a hole through his helmet. Had his head been unprotected, the bolt would have punched into his skull. Nitschke didn't stop to ponder how close he had come to meeting his Maker. He simply grinned and rejoined the workout.[49]

IT'S ALL ABOUT THE PEOPLE

When John Madden was inducted into the Pro Football Hall of Fame in 2006, he vividly described in his induction speech what he imagined would take place in the Hall of Champions every night once the lights were turned out.

"I believe that the busts talk to each other," he said. "I can't wait for that conversation, I really can't. Vince Lombardi, Knute Rockne, Reggie White, Walter Payton, all my ex-players, we'll be there forever and ever talking about whatever. That's what I believe. That's what I think is going to happen, and no one's ever going to talk me out of that."[50]

Wouldn't that be something? Wouldn't those be some fascinating conversations to eavesdrop on? I would love to be a fly on the Hall of Champions wall when Lombardi swaps stories with Knute Rockne and John Madden about how they used their people skills to motivate those championship performances. I'd love to hear from Lombardi's own lips how he needed all of his skills as an amateur psychologist to keep Ray Nitschke on the straight and narrow, to show Jim Taylor how to run to daylight, to prevent Jerry Kramer and Fuzzy Thurston from letting their press clippings go to their heads, and to find the right combination of words to elevate Bart Starr's performance.

Of all the Seven Sides of Leadership that Vince Lombardi possessed, I suspect he enjoyed the people skills side of leadership the most. He was always studying his players, always experimenting with different approaches, always trying to figure out what made them tick, always motivating and making sure they didn't get too high, didn't get too low, but stayed right in that sweet spot of optimal motivation. People skills may well be the most fascinating and fun dimension of leadership, because leadership is all about accomplishing goals through people.

If you want to be a great leader like Vince Lombardi, you've got to focus your attention where he focused his. For Coach Lombardi, it wasn't primarily about X's and O's. It was about *people*.

CHAPTER 4

THE CHARACTER OF VINCE LOMBARDI

Leadership rests not only upon ability, not only upon capacity; having the capacity to lead is not enough. The leader must be willing to use it. His leadership is then based on truth and character. There must be truth in the purpose and willpower in the character.
—Vince Lombardi

He has been nicknamed "St. Vincent of Green Bay," though Coach Vince Lombardi was hardly a "saint" in the conventional sense. As Malcolm Gladwell once characterized him, Vince Lombardi was "brilliant, profane, irascible, charismatic, [and] hot-tempered"—which hardly makes him sound like a role model of character. But in spite of his flaws—and what great human being doesn't have flaws?—I see Vince Lombardi as a man of exemplary moral character.

He had such a reputation as a leader of influence that other great leaders sought him out and looked to him for wisdom. Gladwell writes, "Richard Nixon considered making Lombardi his running mate. John F. Kennedy would call him to talk football. Lombardi and Douglas MacArthur used to discuss Army's football prospects . . . [Lombardi had] the ability to make those who played for him do almost anything and for that he was treated with awe."[51]

Bill Sullivan, one of Coach Lombardi's old Fordham players, was 86 years old when I interviewed him in early 2015. Lombardi recruited Sullivan to Fordham in 1947, where he played as a quarterback and defensive back. Sullivan told me, "Vince Lombardi was an exacting coach because his own discipline was so strong. He showed us what a disciplined life looks like by being one hundred percent ethical and by being a man of his word. He never compromised his character."

Where did Lombardi's gift for inspiring extreme performance come from? I believe it came from two primary qualities of Coach Vince Lombardi—character and love, both his love for his players and their love for him. In fact, after the Green Bay Packers won Super Bowl I, Lombardi designed a special championship ring for his players; on one side of the ring was stamped the word CHARACTER, and on the other side the word LOVE. We will talk about love in chapter 7. For now, let's focus on the character traits of Vince Lombardi and how those traits shaped him as a leader.

THE CHARACTER TRAIT OF FAITH

If there was one dimension of Vince Lombardi's life that defined him above all others, it was his faith. Every day, before leaving the house for work, Lombardi would go to his knees in his bedroom and pray. In his pocket, he carried a string of well-worn rosary beads—he received them as a gift in his prep school days—and he had prayed the rosary many times a day ever since.

There were two books he always kept close at hand: a red leather-bound Catholic Bible and a black leather-bound Maryknoll missal used in the celebration of Catholic Mass. Lombardi kept a card in one of the books as a bookmark, and the card contained a handwritten prayer that read:

> "My God, if I am to die today, or suddenly at any time, I wish to receive this communion as my viaticum. I desire that my last food may be the body and blood of my Savior and Redeemer; my last words, of Jesus, Mary, and Joseph; my last affection, an act of pure love of God and the perfect contrition for my sins; my last consolation, to die in the Holy Grace and in thy Holy Love. Amen."[52]

That term "viaticum" is Latin for "provisions for the journey," and refers to the Eucharist (Holy Communion) as food for the dying person's soul as he begins the journey from this life to the afterlife. Lombardi thought about death and the afterlife every single day of his adult life, and he wanted to be spiritually ready and cleansed of sin whenever the time came to meet his Maker.

Throughout his life, Lombardi attended Mass and received Holy Communion every single day. He was well aware that he was prone to profanity on the football field and in the locker room. Lombardi had a paradoxical view of his volatile nature: he saw it as a weakness and a sin that he needed to confess on a regular basis, yet he also saw his volatility as an asset to effective coaching.

Lombardi's bellowing and cursing sometimes provoked complaints. On one occasion, his administrative assistant, David Slattery, told him about the complaints and asked if he could try to hold it down. "You know, David," Lombardi replied, "I don't understand it. I go to Mass, I never use bad language in my life, until I get to the football season. I'll try to watch it."[53] Biographer David Maraniss wrote, "His daily prayers were an effort to balance the tension between his will to succeed and his desire to be good."[54]

Royce Boyles told me that Bart Starr's roommate Henry Jordan offered a simple theory about why Coach Lombardi was so religious. Bart said, "Henry had a marvelous sense of humor. He said, 'Why hell, if you ever heard him chew our asses out, you'd know why he had to be at church every morning at 7:00 am.'"

Lombardi also prayed daily for his often-troubled marriage to Marie. Though their love for each other was deep and abiding, Vince was not an easy man to be married to. She often resented the amount of time and attention Vince lavished on football at the expense of their marriage. Even when he was home, his mind was often focused on football.

Marie's drinking was also a problem in their marriage. Less than a year after their wedding, Marie suffered a tragic and traumatic miscarriage. She began drinking heavily to numb the pain of that loss. Vince Lombardi was a social drinker who felt he could hold his liquor well, and he was impatient with Marie's "problem," which he considered a weakness. So, from the earliest years of their marriage, the two issues he prayed about most were his temper and his wife's drinking.

I interviewed Pat Richter, the former University of Wisconsin–Madison athletic director who was a wide receiver for the Redskins from 1963 to 1970. He told me, "Vince Lombardi was a man of faith and character who led by example because he had his priorities straight. It was God, family, and team with him. He had a Catholic priest on the Redskins coaching staff. Up at training camp in Carlisle, Pennsylvania, most of the players ended up going to Mass. Until

Coach Lombardi arrived in 1969, I never knew we had so many Catholics on the squad!"

Guard Bob Hyland played college football at Boston College, a private Jesuit school, before being drafted by the Packers in the first round of the 1967 NFL draft. Bob told me, "Coach Lombardi's Catholic upbringing had a lot to do with his effectiveness as a leader. He came through the Jesuit schools and, as a result, religion and family were the foundation blocks of his life. Vince Lombardi was an old-fashioned guy who wanted his family to be proud of him.

"He would go to Mass each morning, then come to practice and share the morning message with us. He was teaching ethics and the principles of good character to us, and I often felt I was back at Boston College, taking another course."

Iggy McPartland played fullback at St. Cecilia High School in Englewood, New Jersey, in 1948, when Vince Lombardi was the head football coach. McPartland saw Coach Lombardi as a role model of character even in those early days of his coaching career. "My two brothers and I were blessed to have such an impressive man in our lives," he said. "Vince studied for the priesthood once and was such a religious man that he influenced my decision to become a priest. I was his 150-pound fullback, and he picked me as one of his captains, but we were all devastated when he left Saints in 1947. I mean, how do you replace Vince Lombardi?"[55]

THE CHARACTER TRAIT OF COMMITMENT

How committed was Vince Lombardi to his role as a football coach? We get a glimpse into the depths of his commitment from his days as the head football coach at St. Cecilia High. As Malcolm Gladwell notes, "Vince Lombardi, perhaps the greatest football coach ever, cut short his honeymoon so he could get back to the high school where he was then coaching before the first fall football practice."[56]

Larry Higgins played fullback for Coach Lombardi at both St. Cecilia High School and Fordham University, where Lombardi also taught science and Latin. Higgins remembers Lombardi as a tough instructor who demanded commitment from his students and players—and got results. By his own admission, Higgins was no standout as a student—yet Lombardi coached the student–athlete to a perfect score in his chemistry exam at Fordham. "I'm not a one-hundred student," Higgins said. "That grade stood out so much for me that it makes my transcript look phony."[57]

In the classroom, Vince Lombardi was a commanding presence. When he was talking, he expected absolute silence and perfect attention—and he would enforce that attention by knocking his Fordham ring against the blackboard. To the students in the classroom, the banging on the blackboard was as loud as a starter's pistol. Everyone in Lombardi's classroom paid attention—or paid the consequences.

Somehow, the story spread around Fordham that Vince Lombardi would lose his temper and throw an eraser at a student. "I think that story is apocryphal," said one of Lombardi's student–players, Joe McPartland. "I had him in class for four years and never heard about it. I guess it's a good anecdote emphasizing his commitment. In the classroom, he just thought you should pursue excellence."[58]

Vince Lombardi wore his own intense commitment on his sleeves, and he expected absolute commitment from his players. "Individual commitment to a group effort," he once said, "is what makes a team work, a company work, a civilization work. The success of the individual is completely subjected to the satisfaction that he receives in being part of the successful whole."[59]

Frank Borman was the head team manager when Vince Lombardi was an assistant coach at West Point. He told me, "Vince Lombardi's intensity was infectious. It just radiated through the ranks. That was his number-one hallmark as a leader. He was intensely committed to winning and excellence. He was quick to praise and quick to criticize, but his players knew that everything he did and said was about being the best, so they respected him and wanted to perform for him."

In 1959, when Lombardi became head coach of the Green Bay Packers—the worst team in the NFL at that time—he took charge of a bunch of undisciplined, out-of-shape players who displayed an attitude of disrespect toward coaches. Lombardi clamped down in a hurry, cutting some players from the roster for bad attitude alone. He told those who remained that he demanded total commitment from his players.

Jerry Kramer recalls the day he and quarterback Joe Francis first met their new head coach:

> Joe and I arrived early for training camp and we decided that we were going to play a little golf . . . Next morning, I was coming down the steps with my golf bag over my shoulder, and there was Lombardi—"Where the hell do you think *you're* going?"
>
> I stammered, "I'm going to go play golf."
>
> "Like hell you are! You're in the dormitory, you make all meals, all meetings, all practices, and observe all curfews just like everybody else!" . . . He didn't mince words. He let you know exactly what was expected of you.

From the very first team meeting, Coach Lombardi said, "If you're not willing to sacrifice, to pay the price, to put the team first and subjugate all your individual needs, wishes, and wants, then get the hell out!" . . .

I was sitting between Bart Starr and Max McGee, and I looked to each side and said, "Surely he can't be this bad, he's just putting on a little front for us." And then we started the grass drills, and he took us through physical conditioning that caused a lot of players to lose consciousness and lose lunch and lose everything else. It was just unbelievable what he was doing to us.[60]

In short, Coach Lombardi demanded total commitment. That first team meeting was burned into the memory of Bart Starr. He recalled:

[Coach Lombardi] looked us in the eye and said, "Gentlemen, we are going to relentlessly chase perfection, knowing full well we will not catch it, because nothing is perfect. In the process we will catch excellence." He paused and said, "I'm not remotely interested in being just good." We knew immediately there would be a change. I called my wife back in Alabama and said, "Honey, we're going to begin to win." It was an absolutely wonderful experience.[61]

Coach Lombardi was totally committed to hard work, sacrifice, and the relentless pursuit of perfection—and he was able by sheer force of will to instill that same character trait of intense commitment into his players. As Donald T. Phillips observes, "When Lombardi confronted a member of his team, he was forcing the individual to think about his personal commitment to the organization and to his own performance."[62] And Coach Lombardi didn't expect anything from his players that he didn't demand from himself. "I don't know how else to live," he once said. "Unless a man believes in himself, and makes a total commitment to his career, and puts everything he has into it—his mind, his body, and his heart—what's life worth to him?"[63]

Lombardi achieved a near-miraculous turnaround in Green Bay, leading the Packers to five NFL Championships and a record of 141-39-4 during his coaching tenure. Then he accepted the head coaching position with another bottom-of-the-barrel team, the Washington Redskins. At a press conference on February 7, 1969, Lombardi promised, "I will demand a commitment to excellence and to victory. That is what life is all about."[64]

THE CHARACTER TRAIT OF SELF-CONTROL

The next trait that defined Coach Lombardi's character was self-control—also called self-discipline. Lombardi himself explained, "A good leader must be harder on himself than anyone else. He must first discipline himself before he can discipline others. A man should not ask others to do things he would not have asked himself to do at one time or another in his life."[65]

Vince Lombardi was intensely competitive. He took losing personally, and it made him angry. There are plenty of occasions when Lombardi's self-control failed him. One of those times was in 1965, after the Packers lost a crucial game to the Rams. Lombardi assembled his team in the locker room and proceeded to rip them up one side and down the other. "You guys don't care if you win or lose," he snarled. "I'm the only one that cares!" And he went on like this, yelling and berating his players for several minutes.

Finally, several players had had enough. Offensive tackle Forrest Gregg leaped to his feet and confronted Coach Lombardi like Fletcher Christian confronting Capt. Bligh on the deck of the *Bounty*—and several other players jumped up and joined in the uprising. The air in the locker room crackled with tension. For several dangerous seconds, the coach and his players stared each other down.

Then Lombardi nodded and said, "All right! That's the kind of attitude I want to see! Who else feels that way?"

Soon, all the Packers were on their feet, shouting their will to win.[66]

To this day, no one knows if Vince Lombardi simply lost his temper when he launched into his angry tirade—or if it was a deliberate strategy to get his players fired up for the next game. I have my own theory. I think he lost his temper—and precisely at that delicate, dangerous moment when everything could have gone horribly wrong, Lombardi found his temper again. He saw a way to take his players' rage and redirect it from him to the next opponent.

I think it takes a lot of self-control, a lot of character to be that self-aware in the heat of the moment. It takes a lot of wisdom to transmute anger into motivation. Lombardi did that on many occasions. He seemed to instinctively sense when he had gone too far, when he had let his anger get the best of him—and he always found a way to bring everyone's emotions (including his own) back into balance.

Learning to control his anger was a lifelong struggle for Coach Lombardi. Many anger-prone people simply say, "Hey, I get mad, that's who I am—deal with it." Not Vince Lombardi. He struggled with his anger. He prayed daily for wisdom and strength to manage his anger. He even apologized for his anger.

Jerry Kramer told me that, in spite of Lombardi's often harsh and volatile personality, "he could also be very gentle and understanding. He was observant, and he was sensitive to his players' emotions. He'd try to smooth things over, clap you on the back, and sometimes he'd even come right out and say, 'Jerry, I'm sorry. I shouldn't have said that.' That didn't happen often, but it happened."

And Pat Peppler, who was the director of player personnel with the Packers, told me, "One day during our lunch break, Vince came over to me and said, 'Pat, you never seem to get upset over anything. Nothing ever bothers you. What is it with you?' He seemed to want to learn my secret. So I told him, 'Well, Coach, I have five kids and a high-maintenance wife—so compared to that, this football thing is a piece of cake.' He just shook his head and walked away."

The point is not that Coach Lombardi practiced perfect self-control. He didn't. What's important is that Lombardi was always trying, always praying for help and wisdom, always eager to learn and grow and improve his character. He considered his character a work-in-progress, and he never stopped trying to improve it.

THE CHARACTER TRAIT OF MENTAL TOUGHNESS

Mental toughness is not just one trait, but a category of traits that includes the will to win, the willingness to make personal sacrifices and deny the self, and the will to persevere through pain, opposition, and obstacles to achieve a worthwhile goal. Coach Lombardi said this about mental toughness: "Mental toughness is many things and rather difficult to explain. Its qualities are sacrifice and self-denial. Also, most importantly, it is combined with a perfectly disciplined will that refuses to give in. It's a state of mind—you could call it character in action."[67]

Vince Lombardi exemplified mental toughness when he was a guard on Fordham's offensive line and a member of the famed "Seven Blocks of Granite." Though Lombardi was undersized at 172 pounds, no one dared underestimate his ferocity and toughness. In that 1936 game in which a 215-pound tackle elbowed him in the mouth, Lombardi spit teeth and blood and kept playing, kept battling that tackle, play after play. He never forgot what his father taught him: "Hurt is in the mind." Years later, recalling that game, he said, "I certainly was hurting in my mind!"[68]

Lombardi carried his commitment to mental toughness into his coaching career. At St. Cecilia, his team practiced on a field without lights. When it began to get dark, he'd have his players and their friends line up their cars and turn on their headlights so the workout could continue.

During games, when the opposing teams were taking a rest and drinking water, Coach Lombardi had his players doing jumping jacks and push-ups on the field. He would tell his players, "You can break the heart of the other team. You can show them indestructability." And that's exactly what his players proceeded to do.

One of Coach Lombardi's St. Cecilia players, Joe McPartland, tells about a time his brother Frank, a lineman, was going through a workout. Coach Lombardi didn't think Frank was hitting his opponent hard enough. So Lombardi got into a stance opposite Frank and said, "Okay, come on! Hit me!" Frank launched at Lombardi, but Lombardi blocked him and pushed them back. "Not good enough! Try it again!" So Frank launched at Lombardi again— and smashed him in the face. Lombardi's nose began bleeding— profusely. Lombardi laughed. "Now you've got it, Frank! I like that!"

That's how Lombardi taught mental toughness to his players at St. Cecilia.[69]

Years later, as coach of the Green Bay Packers, Vince Lombardi would urge his players to demonstrate mental toughness, to persevere through adversity, and to play through the pain. Some of Coach Lombardi's critics thought he was cruel and unfeeling and that he pushed his players too hard.

One of those critics was *Esquire* sportswriter Leonard Shecter. Lombardi gave Shecter unprecedented access to the Packers facility, personnel, and sidelines. Shecter produced a profile of Lombardi for the December 1967 issue—and the piece left Coach Lombardi devastated. The evening of the day the issue hit the stands, Coach Lombardi went out to dinner with friends. He took a copy of the *Esquire* issue with him to dinner and read a few passages, red-faced and blinking behind his glasses. Here's an excerpt:

> There is a pileup and out of the bottom of the pile comes a cry that has been torn out of the man's throat, a shriek of agony. It's Jerry Moore, a rookie guard, who hasn't learned he is not supposed to cry in pain. The pile untangles and Moore is left writhing on the ground, his hands grabbing at a knee which is swelling so fast that in another minute the doctor will have to cut his pants leg to get at it. "Get up!" Lombardi bawls, the thick cords on his heavy, sun-browned neck standing out with the effort. "Get up! Get up off the *ground.*" The sight has insulted him. He is outraged. "You're not hurt. *You're not hurt.*"[70]

The *Esquire* article was a hatchet job, distorted and one-sided. Shecter didn't just report what he saw but pretended to peer into Lombardi's motivations and motives, deliberately portraying Lombardi as some sort of sadist. As Lombardi himself put it, the piece made him look like a Mafia boss. After Lombardi read the passages to his dinner companions, he asked in a wounded voice, "Am I like this? Am I really like this?"[71]

Those who knew Coach Lombardi best were quick to leap to his defense. Jerry Kramer gave interviews in which he was quick to point out that there was much more to Coach Vincent Lombardi than the rough side of his tongue. The *Esquire* piece, Kramer said, "gave a distorted picture of the man; it showed only one of his many sides." While it's true, Kramer added, that Lombardi drove his players hard, he drove himself and his coaching staff even harder, usually working 15-hour days, seven days a week during the season. "On an hourly basis," Kramer said, "a Green Bay coach earns less than a Green Bay garbage man."

Sports writers and columnists who knew Lombardi well were also quick to come to his defense, including Howard Cosell, Red Smith, and Jim Murray. With the support of his players, coaches, and friends in the media, Lombardi was eventually able to shrug off the *Esquire* hit job. But it hurt him deeply and for a very long time.[72] The pain of being misjudged in the media can hurt worse than a smash to the mouth—and it takes mental toughness to get through both kinds of pain.

Vince Lombardi set an example of mental toughness that inspired his own players to sacrifice, to deny themselves, and to play through the pain in order to achieve championships. His players knew that their coach had never demanded anything from them that he hadn't demanded of himself—and more.

As former Packers wide receiver Bob Long told me, "Vince Lombardi had old-school values. He loved his veterans and he wasn't always patient with the mistakes our rookies made. You had to be

THE CHARACTER OF VINCE LOMBARDI

mentally tough to play for Vince Lombardi. You couldn't make mental mistakes."

Coach Lombardi had a lot to say about mental toughness. Here are a few of his most memorable sayings:

> *"You never win a game unless you beat the guy in front of you. The score on the board doesn't mean a thing. That's for the fans. You've got to win the war with the man in front of you. You've got to get your man."*

> *"It's not whether you get knocked down, it's whether you get up."*

> *"The harder you work, the harder it is to surrender."*

> *"Once you learn to quit, it becomes a habit."*

> *"Anything is yours if you want it bad enough."*

> *"Winning is not everything—but making effort to win is."*

> *"I firmly believe that any man's finest hour, the greatest fulfillment of all that he holds dear, is the moment when he has worked his heart out in a good cause and lies exhausted on the field of battle—victorious."*

If you want to understand who Coach Lombardi was and what made him successful, you'll find a lot of it wrapped up in the array of character traits he called "mental toughness."

THE CHARACTER TRAIT OF OPEN-MINDEDNESS

Lori Keck told me how she got the job as Vince Lombardi's secretary—and the story reveals a Lombardi character trait that I call "open-mindedness" or "approachability." Lori recalled, "It was 1961, and I had just graduated from Badger Business College. The first job that cropped up was Prange's Department Store. I was a secretary in the buyer's office, and I hated it. While I worked at Prange's, I told the employment agency I wanted another job. Finally, the agency called and said, 'The Packers are looking for a girl'—that was the terminology in those days. I had lived all my life in Sturgeon Bay, forty-five miles away, so my first question was, 'What are the Packers?' They said, 'A professional football team.' I was twenty years old, and the first thing I thought of was, 'Well, men in tight pants! Let's go check it out!'

"After a preliminary interview with Vern Llewellyn, the business manager, I went back for an interview with Lombardi himself. This was soon after the Packers had lost to the Philadelphia Eagles in the NFL Championship Game. So Lombardi was famous in the sports world but not yet the legend he would soon become. I didn't know Lombardi from Adam, so I went into that interview with a casual, almost flippant attitude. Instead of being intimidated by Lombardi, like most people were, I was outspoken and confident. I said exactly what I thought.

"I would later find out that very few people spoke their minds freely around Vince Lombardi. Most people just 'yessed' him. But I found that he actually *liked* people who would tell him the truth, as long as they were respectful. He must have liked it that I spoke my mind and wasn't afraid of him. He didn't ask me to prove my dictation or typing skills, but he did say, 'Do you mind if I call Jerry

Atkinson?' Mr. Atkinson was the president of H. C. Prange, and he was also on the Packers board. I said, 'No, I don't mind, but I'm sure he doesn't know me.'

"After the interview, I walked home, because I didn't have a car. About fifteen minutes after I got home, Lombardi called and told me I had the job.

"I didn't know the first thing about football. After attending my first Packers game, I went into the office on Monday morning and we had our coffee break at ten. Over coffee, the other girls asked me, 'Do you have any questions about the game?' I said, 'Yeah. What's a down?" I had watched the whole game and didn't know what a down was.

"Our offices at that time were in the Downtowner Motel. We had very small offices. The reception area, where the office girls were, was right next to Lombardi's office. One day, Lombardi called Ray Nitschke in. I was at the mimeograph machine, next to the back door of Lombardi's office. All of a sudden, I heard the most awful shouting and swearing! I had never heard Vince Lombardi sound off before, and it scared me. It turned out that Nitschke had been drinking the night before, and he threw a glass of whiskey in a woman's face. It got back to Lombardi, as all things did. And Lombardi was saying (this is a mild version), 'Dammit, Ray, if you can't handle your drinks, don't drink!'

"And that was my introduction to how volatile Vince Lombardi could be. He was never that way toward me, but he was a demanding boss. You can do something wrong once, but don't make the same mistake twice or you're gone. And you wanted to do everything right so you wouldn't get yelled at.

"The one criticism I had of him was that, if he was chewing somebody out, it didn't matter where he was or who was present.

I would have preferred that he take that person into his office and handle the matter privately. But of course, he was so loud that it wouldn't have made any difference.

"Even though Lombardi was demanding, the place wasn't ruled by fear. The Packers office had a family atmosphere. A lot of companies say, 'We run our business like a family,' but it's really just talk. Lombardi didn't talk about it, but he was very family oriented, and the organization reflected his personality. One time, my mother was in the hospital and I asked Lombardi for time off to be with her. He said, 'You go, you do what you have to do.' He believed you should put family first, so if you had a family crisis, he was very kind and understanding about it. That made the Packers office a great place to work.

"It was easy to take dictation from Lombardi, because he would always add the punctuation, spell all the proper names, and I never had to question anything. He liked to use Latin phrases in his correspondence. I knew nothing about Latin, of course, so I was always looking things up in the dictionary.

"One time he used an odd word that I didn't know, so just to make sure, I looked the word up in two dictionaries, and I was sure I had spelled it right. He proofread the letter, and said, 'That word is spelled wrong.' I said, 'No, it's not.' 'Yes, it is.' 'I looked it up in two dictionaries.' He said, 'I don't care, that's wrong.' Well, I looked at the paper and saw that I had transposed two letters when I typed it. So he was never wrong.

"Another time, he called me in to take a letter. I had my pad and was taking it down in shorthand. He started dictating, and he hadn't finished the second sentence before I realized—*This is his resignation letter.* There had been rumors he was thinking of leaving, but I had hoped they weren't true. Now there was no doubt. Tears started rolling down my face, and I didn't think I could get through the letter. Then the phone rang. I got up, went in the bathroom, dried my eyes, and composed myself. Then I went back and finished taking the letter.

"When he had finished, I asked him if I could go to Washington with him. He said no, part of the deal of getting out of his contract with Green Bay was that he couldn't recruit personnel from the Packers for a year—and that included office personnel.

"I stayed for a while after Lombardi left, but the Packers organization wasn't the same anymore. I wanted to move to Milwaukee, because I had a sister there. I went on about thirty job interviews, but nothing clicked. Then the employment agency sent me to apply at the Milwaukee Brewers office—and I got the job as secretary to the team president, Bud Selig. There was no interview. I met Selig the day I started work. It turned out he hired me purely because of my Lombardi background. He told me, 'If you're good enough for Lombardi, you're good enough for me.'

"I ended up working for Selig for thirty-seven and a half years, including his years as the commissioner of baseball. I couldn't have asked for two better bosses than Vince Lombardi and Bud Selig. I really lucked out."

I was glad Lori Keck shared her story with me. She revealed an insight into Lombardi's character that none of my other interviews uncovered: Vince Lombardi was surprisingly approachable and open minded. Lombardi had interviewed a number of applicants besides Lori Keck, yet after just one meeting with her, he was sold. He offered her the job that very same day. What was it about her job interview that appealed to him? She spoke her mind. She was not intimidated. She leveled with Lombardi.

Great leaders don't avoid the hard truths. They give their people permission to speak freely—because accurate information is the lifeblood of leadership. As a leader, don't surround yourself with "yes-men." Be approachable. Be open-minded. Always be receptive to the truth.

THE CHARACTER TRAITS OF INTEGRITY AND FAIRNESS

Sportswriter Bud Lea was born and raised in Green Bay and spent more than five decades covering the Packers for the *Milwaukee Sentinel* and Packer Plus. He told me, "Vince Lombardi could have been successful in any field of endeavor. If he'd gone into politics, he could have been elected to any office. If he'd gone into the priesthood in the Catholic Church, he could have been a bishop or even a cardinal. His strength of character made you trust him. You could believe what he said, you could trust his integrity. And one more thing—if he was coaching today, he'd be just as outstanding a football coach as he was in the 1960s. The game may have changed, the rules are different, but the qualities that made Lombardi a great leader still hold true today as they did in the Lombardi Era."

And Hall of Fame wide receiver Charley Taylor of the Redskins told me, "Coach Lombardi was a man of his word. In fact, his word was gospel. He would never lie to you. We played our hearts out for him because we believed in him." Taylor had played five seasons for the perennially losing Redskins before Lombardi took over as coach. "My first day of practice for Coach Lombardi, we were doing the nutcracker drill. First time I tried it, I broke my right hand. Coach Lombardi came over and said, 'I'm going to make you the best one-handed pass catcher in the league.'" That season, Taylor caught 71 passes—second-best in the league.

Packers running back Ben Wilson's assessment of Coach Lombardi was surprisingly similar to Charley Taylor's. Wilson told me, "Coach Lombardi was extremely fair and consistent. If he told you something today, it was gospel. He wouldn't tell you something different tomorrow. Coach was not a respecter of persons. He didn't show favoritism. He was very fair to me and to all of us."

And Packers safety Willie Wood called Coach Lombardi "perhaps the fairest person I ever met."[73]

Was Lombardi's integrity completely without blemish? Well, let me put it this way: Coach Lombardi was not above stretching the truth a tad for the sake of enlarging his legend. Royce Boyles showed me Coach Lombardi's bio from the *1967 Packers Media Guide*. One paragraph begins, "After earning his Law Degree from Fordham, Lombardi coached and taught . . . "

Whoa! Did you catch that? You may remember that young Vince Lombardi *did* enroll in Fordham's law school—but he quit after one semester. He didn't earn a degree in law. Now, Lombardi didn't write that erroneous bio himself—but as Royce told me, "Lombardi was on top of every detail, and he undoubtedly checked his bio in the *Yearbook*. As his secretary, Lori Keck, will tell you, Lombardi's proofreading skills were unmatched. I'm sure he spotted that mistake about his 'law degree,' but he probably figured, 'Why correct the error if doing so would only diminish the legend?'"

But there were other areas of integrity and character where Lombardi set a powerful example. As biographer David Maraniss observed, "Race was an issue that revealed the integrity of Lombardi's character."[74] Vince Lombardi coached the Packers during the turbulent Sixties, the era of the civil rights movement. Lombardi had many African American players on his team, and he was fond of saying that in the Packers organization, there was no black, no white, just Packers green.

On one occasion, early in his tenure as Packers head coach, he called his players together on the practice field and lectured them on team unity. He said, "If I ever hear"—and he listed several racial slurs—"regardless of who you are, you are through with me. You can't play for me if you have any kind of prejudice." Coach Lombardi also made it known in the community that if any tavern or restaurant in Green Bay discriminated against his black players, that establishment would be off-limits to his white players as well.

In 1963, the Packers drafted defensive end Lionel Aldridge, a standout player from Utah State. There was just one problem: Aldridge was an African American engaged to a white Mormon girl. Interracial marriage was practically unheard of in the early 1960s— and the NFL was dead-set against their marriage. Aldridge passed away in 1998, but I had the privilege of interviewing Vicky Aldridge Nelson. "When Lionel and I were going to get married," she told me, "he went to ask Coach Lombardi if he'd still have a job if he married me. Another player had already been blackballed from the league for an interracial marriage, so Lionel knew his football career was at risk.

"Coach Lombardi told Lionel he didn't care who he married as long as he played good football and kept his nose clean. When NFL commissioner Pete Rozelle heard about our impending marriage, he came to Green Bay and talked to Coach Lombardi in person. The coach told Rozelle, 'This is my team and I can do what I want with my players.' Lombardi hated racial prejudice, and he was risking his own career by taking a stand for his beliefs. But the league backed down, and Lombardi prevailed. Watching Coach Lombardi take a stand against prejudice made me a stronger person and served as an example of moral courage."

Though Lombardi could rightfully claim to be color-blind (he was color-blind physically as well as metaphorically), the Packers often had to play in cities where Jim Crow was alive and well. All Lombardi wanted to do was coach his players and win some football games—but the times in which he lived forced him to become a warrior for the civil rights of his players. When playing exhibition games in the South, Lombardi refused to split up his team, sending his white players and African American players to different hotels.

Vince Lombardi was not a perfect man, but he was a good man with solid character. His durable character helped to make him a leader of enduring influence. Cornerback Herb Adderley played most of his career with the Green Bay Packers. He told me that the key to Lombardi's influence was his character, then he added, "My father and Vince Lombardi were the two most influential men in my life—but I don't think of my father every minute of the day." I don't think Herb Adderley is saying he *literally* thinks about Lombardi every minute; rather, he's underscoring the profound impact Lombardi had on his life after football. In my interviews with Lombardi's old players, it has been fascinating to hear so many of them express gratitude for Lombardi's influence on their daily lives.

Jerry Kramer told me that Coach Lombardi had a seven-point roadmap to success that he shared with his players. "You can't argue with Vince Lombardi's fundamental principles of success," he said. "Coach Lombardi's seven key points were:

1. Preparation.

2. Commitment.

3. Discipline (do things right all the time).

4. Perseverance.

5. Character.

6. Pride.

7. The Perfectly Disciplined Will.

"That was Coach Lombardi's way of getting us to reach for perfection. We were always striving to achieve that perfect game, and though we'd always fall short, we always kept reaching. You never saw the Packers doing a lot of celebrating when we scored. There was no reason to celebrate, because we hadn't achieved our goal of a perfect game. He told us that the rings and money don't last, but the will to win and excel will endure."

In a *New York Times* op-ed piece, Kramer said, "The lessons Lombardi taught were only incidentally about football. They were about life." Kramer talked about the impact of Coach Lombardi's influence. Kramer's teammate and roommate, Willie Davis, was working on his MBA from the University of Chicago at the same time he was playing with the Packers. At one point, Davis became discouraged and nearly quit school because he found it hard to keep up with his studies while playing in the NFL. A lot of coaches would have preferred that their players focus solely on the game, but Coach Lombardi encouraged Willie Davis to stay in school. Lombardi believed Davis would have stronger character (and thus be a better player) if he persevered in his studies and didn't quit.

Kramer also gives Coach Lombardi credit for building strong character and strong values into other teammates who later went on to do well in the business world. In those days, there were no multimillion dollar contracts, and NFL players didn't get rich playing football. But many of Coach Lombardi's players—Max McGee, Paul Hornung, Bart Starr, Doug Hart, and others—became wealthy and successful because they learned life lessons from their coach. All of these players, Kramer says, "are still driven by Lombardi—not because he ranted and raved but because he wanted desperately to see us do well."[75]

Former Packers defensive back Dale Hackbart agrees with Kramer's assessment. "My time with Vince Lombardi laid the foundation for my long career in sales. After I retired from the NFL, I got in the tire business in Colorado. The number one thing in my new career was preparation. I had to prepare my sales calls, study my competition, study my clients, and know their likes and dislikes. Coach Lombardi had drilled into me such values as the importance of never being late for a meeting, being self-disciplined and self-motivated, perseverance and mental toughness through adversity, and staying on top of your game, 24/7. At the time, I thought he was teaching about football. But looking back, I realize he gave me all the essential skills I needed to succeed in business and in life."

Running back Jim Taylor played ten seasons in the NFL, nine with the Green Bay Packers, and one with the New Orleans Saints expansion franchise. He was part of four Green Bay championship teams—1961, 1962, 1965, and 1966—and was the top rusher in Super Bowl I. Jim Taylor gives Coach Lombardi much of the credit for his success both on and off the field. "Coach Lombardi taught us so much about being unselfish, about persevering through adversity, and about being a good teammate. He instilled this in us, and it still carries over into our daily lives. Lombardi wanted us to be great not only as football players but as human beings, and he taught us to care about people who were less fortunate. For the past fifty years, I've been trying to live up to the standards he set for us. My heart and soul is wrapped up in my charity work, and I want to honor Lombardi's memory by making a contribution that will make a difference in people's lives."

Vince Lombardi once said, "I don't build character. I eliminate the people who don't have it." Well, the second part of that statement is true. Lombardi did eliminate players who just didn't have the strong character traits to build a winning team.

But he's mistaken about the first part of that statement. Ask any of Coach Lombardi's old players (and in the course of writing this book, I think I asked every one still living) and they will tell you that Vince Lombardi not only built character, but he also exemplified character, and he led by the influence of his character. Coach Vince Lombardi's leadership legacy is a legacy of character. As Jerry Kramer told me, "Vince Lombardi didn't just coach football. He coached life. He made every one of us better than we thought we could be."

Before serving as the ninth commissioner of Major League Baseball, Bud Selig was the owner and president of the Milwaukee Brewers. Selig and his ownership group purchased the bankrupt Seattle Pilots and renamed them the Milwaukee Brewers. Bud told me, "On April 1, 1970, when we acquired the baseball team for Milwaukee, the first telegram of congratulations I received was from Vince Lombardi. He was one of the most remarkable man I've ever known—a role model of leadership through his inspiring words and his actions on and off the field. He set an example of leadership for all of us to follow. When you study great lives and you want to understand the kind of character that makes a leader great, you can't do much better than Vince Lombardi."

CHAPTER 5

THE COMPETENCE OF VINCE LOMBARDI

The spirit, the will to win and the will to excel, these are the things that endure and these are the qualities that are so much more important than any of the events that occasion them.
—Vince Lombardi[76]

The Packers have been in Green Bay, Wisconsin, since the team was founded by Curly Lambeau in 1919. The team is named for its first sponsor, the Indian Packing Company, which employed Lambeau and contributed $500 for football equipment and uniforms. The Packers were granted a franchise in the National Football League in 1921, one year after the NFL was founded, and the team has played in its original city longer than any other NFL franchise.

Green Bay claimed its first NFL title in 1929, a season that registered an undefeated 12-0-1 record, including eight shutouts. Green Bay won the title again in 1930 and 1931 and amassed a streak of 30 consecutive home wins—an NFL record that still stands today. Additional NFL titles followed in 1936, 1939, and 1944. The era from 1945 through 1958 was a period of decline for the Packers. The absolute nadir for the once-storied franchise was the disastrous 1958 season under head coach Ray "Scooter" McLean, whose 1–10–1 record was the absolute worst in Packer history.

THEN CAME LOMBARDI.

Hired as the Packers new head coach and general manager on February 2, 1959, Vince Lombardi arrived with a specific goal. He was going to turn the absolute worst, bottom-of-the-barrel team in the NFL into a championship team. Hardly anyone believed he could do it. The sports writers didn't believe it. The fans didn't believe it. And the Packers themselves didn't believe it.

Why should anyone believe that Vince Lombardi, whose only head-coaching job had been at a tiny Catholic high school, would unerringly guide the Packers through championship after championship? Expectations could not have been lower.

But the Packers got off to a great start in their first season under Coach Lombardi, winning their first three games. They stumbled, losing five in a row, then recovered to win their last four games for a record of 7-5-0. It was the Packers' first winning season since 1947—and Vince Lombardi was honored as NFL Coach of the Year.

The following year, 1960, the Packers won the NFL West, and advanced to the NFL Championship Game against the Philadelphia Eagles. The game was played the day after Christmas 1960 at Franklin Field in Philadelphia. I was home on Christmas break from my junior year at Wake Forest, so my dad and I got tickets and went to the game—I still have the program among my sports souvenirs. (That was the second time I saw Lombardi in person. The first time, in November 1947, I was seven years old and my dad took me to see Lafayette College at Fordham. Lombardi was an assistant at Fordham, and I remember the game—Fordham lost 7 to 0.)

The Western Conference champion Packers came into the game with an 8-4 record, making their first NFL championship appearance since 1944. Though favored to win, the Packers trailed 10 to 6 at the half but pulled to within four in the fourth quarter.

Trailing 17 to 13 in the closing seconds of the game, the Packers reached the Eagles' 22-yard line. Bart Starr took the snap and lobbed a short pass to fullback Jim Taylor. There was only one Eagle defender between Taylor and the goal line—but that defender was "Concrete Charlie," Eagles linebacker Chuck Bednarik. He tackled Taylor on the 9-yard line and held him down, making sure the Packers had no time for another play. When time expired, Bednarik said, "You can get up now, Taylor. This game's over."[77]

The Packers' quest for an NFL championship ended nine yards short of the goal line. It was a bitter defeat for Coach Lombardi. He later met with the media and took the blame: "I lost the game, not my players," he said.

Later, in the locker room, Lombardi made a vow to his players—and one of the players who was in the room that day was wide receiver Boyd Dowler, who played 11 seasons in Green Bay. Boyd told me, "After we lost to the Eagles, some of the guys were cussing, pounding on things, throwing things around. A big loss, a championship loss, is horrible. Coach Lombardi came into the locker room and gathered us together. 'I want you to go home and think about what happened,' he said. 'I want you to learn from this. Come back in the fall and get ready to win. As long as I am here, we're never going to lose another postseason game.' And we never did."

The following year, 1961, the Packers again played in the title game, this time against Lombardi's old team, the New York Giants.

The Packers routed the Giants, 37-0, and Green Bay earned the sobriquet of "Titletown." In the 1962 NFL Championship Game, the Packers again defeated the Giants, this time by a score of 16-7. The next two seasons, the Packers fell short of the playoffs but returned to the NFL championship game in 1965, defeating the Cleveland Browns, 23-12.

In the 1966 season, the Packers went 12-2 through the regular season and capped it off with a victory in the first-ever Super Bowl, defeating the Kansas City Chiefs 35-10.

The 1967 season was famous for the legendary "Ice Bowl," the 1967 NFL Championship Game. There, the Packers welcomed the Dallas Cowboys to the coldest conditions in NFL history. After clinching the NFL title, the Packers went on to defeat the Oakland Raiders of the American Football League 33-14 in Super Bowl II.

The following season, Lombardi stepped down as head coach, remaining as general manager for the 1968 season. He left in 1969 to become head coach and minority owner of the Washington Redskins. After just one season with the Redskins—the team's first winning season in 14 years—Lombardi died of cancer on September 3, 1970.

In honor of Lombardi's huge impact on the game during a decade-long head-coaching career, the NFL fittingly named the Super Bowl trophy the Vince Lombardi Trophy. The decade of the 1960s would forever be known in the sports world as the Lombardi Era.

AN INTELLECTUAL TOOLBOX

Competence is the fifth of the Seven Sides of Leadership, and the competence of Coach Vince Lombardi stands out as one of his most distinctive leadership traits. Yet in my study of Vince Lombardi's leadership life, I find that his depth of competence has been greatly underappreciated by both his admirers and detractors.

There is a stereotype of athletes and coaches in the public mind as "dumb jocks" who have no knowledge of, or interest in, anything but sports. A friend of mine once dubbed me a "Renaissance jock" because of my wide-ranging interests in history, philosophy, theology, business, government, and other fields in addition to sports. But if anyone truly deserves the appellation of "Renaissance jock" (next to the great Coach John Wooden), it is Vince Lombardi.

Like Coach Wooden, Coach Lombardi was a well-educated, well-read man with a wide range of interests. Like Wooden, Lombardi saw himself as a teacher first, a coach second. In addition to coaching sports at St. Cecilia and Fordham, Lombardi taught such subjects as chemistry, physics, biology, and Latin, and his students all said that he was well versed in those subjects and highly competent to teach. In fact, his students said that his classes were difficult to pass because he was a demanding instructor.

I believe the best leaders tend to be "polymaths," people with knowledge, interest, and expertise that span a variety of subjects. The broader the scope of your knowledge, the greater the depth of insight you have to draw on when solving problems and making decisions. Great leadership insight can come from anywhere, and the more we know, the more competent we become.

Vince Lombardi had a depth of knowledge that enabled him to find "cross-matrix" solutions to problems. When Coach Lombardi needed to find the right message for an inspiring halftime speech, he could draw upon his deep knowledge of the Bible or military history to supply a powerful analogy. When he needed to find the key to motivating Jerry Kramer or Paul Hornung, he could draw upon his keen understanding of human psychology. When he needed to explain the mechanics of the Packers Sweep to his players, he could draw upon years of teaching the laws of physics in the classroom.

It is said that "to a man with a hammer, every problem is a nail." Coach Vince Lombardi's intellectual toolbox was deep and contained many tools. His breadth and depth of knowledge equipped him to apply solutions that might not respond well to a hammer. While a sledge hammer might work just fine with Ray Nitschke, Coach Lombardi needed the finest, gentlest grade of steel wool to deal with Max McGee. Vince Lombardi's broad intellect gave him the tools he needed in any coaching situation.

Leadership author Warren Bennis observed, "Mastery, absolute competence, is mandatory for a leader."[78] Coach Vince Lombardi exemplified his leadership mastery by inspiring the Green Bay Packers to function at a consistently high level of success. "Competence goes beyond words," John C. Maxwell wrote in *The 21 Indispensable Qualities of a Leader*. "It's the leader's ability to say it, plan it, and do it in such a way that others know that you know how—and know that they want to follow you."[79] Let's look at some of the specific areas of competence that made Coach Vince Lombardi such a competent leader.

COMPETENT TO COMPETE

In *Rozelle: A Biography*, sports journalist Jerry Izenberg writes that one of NFL commissioner Pete Rozelle's greatest challenges in the 1960s was dealing with "the volatile psyche of Vince Lombardi." Before any game, Lombardi had a tendency to become hyper-competitive in every area of his life. At such times, Izenberg notes, the Packers coach "generally had all the restraint of a falling safe."

Lombardi would even become intensely competitive with his own grandson, as Izenberg records:

> I remember his wife, Marie, telling me of a day he played marbles with his young grandson in the Lombardi living room. When the kid began to cry and Marie asked him why, he said, "Grandpa is winning all my marbles."
>
> "Vince," she whispered, "he's only a baby. Let him win once."
>
> "Mind your business, Marie," he said.

Jerry Izenberg concluded, "Competition of any kind was his emotional heartbeat."[80]

Running back Chuck Mercein told me about an incident he experienced soon after joining the Packers midway through the 1967 season. Green Bay had already clinched the division title and went to Los Angeles to play the Rams. Though the game was nationally televised, it was meaningless in terms of the standings and the playoffs. But it was anything but "meaningless" to Vince Lombardi.

"We lost the game on a blocked kick, of all things," Mercein said. "Coach Lombardi was absolutely livid about the loss. It didn't matter a whit to him that we had already clinched our division. It was a game, and he expected us to win. There was nothing more important to him than winning. As he had reminded us all week, the game was on national television, and he damn well wanted us to perform at our best on a national stage. Watching Coach Lombardi, I learned what it really means to be competitive."

Look closely at the word *competence* and you find another equally important word embedded there—*compete*. When you are a leader of proven competence, you give your followers the assurance that you can make them competitive—and you will lead them to victory. Competence is much more than mere knowledge or skill. Competent people exemplify competitive drive. Some people are born with a naturally competitive spirit, but competitiveness can also be a learned, acquired trait. Competitiveness is a natural and positive urge—we all want to win. The competitive urge only becomes destructive when people decide they want to win at all costs, without regard to the rules of fair play and the laws of God and man.

Leaders have a responsibility to exemplify healthy competitiveness. Leaders set the tone for the team or organization, and followers tend to mold themselves to the character of the leader. So leaders, if they want to build an organization that competes, must set an example of competitive excellence. Raising the bar of excellence benefits everyone both within the organization and without.

Vince Lombardi's competitive spirit is evident in the lessons he taught his players and in his quotations, which have been preserved for us. Here are a few of Vince Lombardi's thoughts on competitiveness:

"The spirit, the will to win and the will to excel—these are the things that endure and these are the qualities that are so much more important than any of the events that occasion them."

"Brains without competitive hearts are rudderless."[81]

"Football isn't a contact sport; it's a collision sport. Dancing is a contact sport."[82]

"The trouble with me is that my ego just can't accept a loss. I suppose that if I were more perfectly adjusted I could toss off defeat but my name is on this ball club. Thirty-six men publicly reflect me and reflect on me, and it's a matter of my pride."[83]

"I used to run the Green Bay Packers. At first, we didn't win. Later on, we won our fair share. Still never as many as I wanted. Which was all of them."[84]

Coach Lombardi once gave a speech entitled "What It Takes to Be Number One," which expressed his views on competition. Here's an excerpt from that speech:

> Winning is not a sometime thing; it's an all the time thing. You don't win once in a while; you don't do things right once in a while; you do them right all of the time. Winning is a habit. Unfortunately, so is losing . . . It is and always has been an American zeal to be first in anything we do, and to win, and to win, and to win . . .

> Running a football team is no different than running any other kind of organization—an army, a political party, or a business. The principles are the same. The object is to win—to beat the other guy. Maybe that sounds hard or cruel. I don't think it is . . . The object is to win fairly, squarely, by the rules—but to win.[85]

One of the keys to Coach Lombardi's effectiveness as a leader was his ability to communicate his intense competitiveness to his players, so that *his* will to win became *their* will to win. Bart Starr recalls, "I wasn't mentally tough before I met Coach Lombardi. I hadn't reached the point where I refused to accept second-best . . . Coach Lombardi gave me that. He taught me that you must have a flaming desire to win. It's got to dominate all your waking hours. It can't ever wane. It's got to glow in you all the time."[86]

But, Starr is quick to add, Lombardi's competitiveness was *not* the win-at-all-costs caricature so often presented in the media.

"Winning to Lombardi was neither everything nor the only thing," Starr said. "He was more interested in seeing us make the effort to be our best. If we did, he knew that winning would usually take care of itself."[87]

Starr made reference to a famous quote that is often attributed to Coach Lombardi: "Winning isn't everything; it's the only thing." This statement actually originated with UCLA Bruins football coach Red Sanders, though Lombardi is said to have repeated it on a few occasions. When speaking on the record, Coach Lombardi adopted a more nuanced version: "Winning isn't everything—the will to win is the only thing,"[88] which demonstrated his awareness that a win-at-all-costs aggressiveness brings out the worst in people.

A number of years ago in my home state of Florida, a youth football team, all fifth-graders, played undefeated all season but lost the state championship game. As a result, this team took second place in the entire state. At a banquet for the team at the end of the season, each player received a plaque. Inscribed on the plaque was a quote by Vince Lombardi:

> There is no room for second place. There is only one place in my game, and that's first place. I have finished second twice in my time at Green Bay, and I don't ever want to finish second again. There is a second place bowl game, but it is a game for losers played by losers.[89]

Now, those words are perfectly appropriate for Coach Lombardi to deliver to a team of paid professional football players. But that's an inappropriate and harmful message to send to a team of fifth-graders who should be learning to love the game, play fair, and learn lessons in character. Adults should never convey to kids that they are "losers" if they fail to win the state championship. Vince Lombardi never would have made that speech to children after a painful loss, and he would be horrified to know his words were misused that way.

(If you are involved in coaching youth sports, I urge you to look into the Positive Coaching Alliance at www.positivecoach.org/. The PCA is dedicated to providing all youth and high school athletes "a positive, character-building youth sports experience." The organization offers many resources to help you become a better coach and a positive role model for your players.)

Intense competitiveness—the will to win, the drive toward excellence—is the foundation of a leader's competence to lead. All of your other skills are built on that foundation.

COMPETENT TO PLAN AND PREPARE

Inspirational speaker–author Frank Candy shared a boyhood memory of Vince Lombardi with me. Frank grew up in East Cleveland, Ohio, and played youth football. His father had once arranged for Lombardi (who was then an assistant coach with the New York Giants) to speak at an event in Cleveland. When Lombardi took the head-coaching job in Green Bay, Frank and his dad became big-time Packers fans.

In September 1962, Frank's dad drove his son 400 miles to Milwaukee to watch the Packers play the St. Louis Cardinals. They arrived at Milwaukee County Stadium before sunrise, and the parking lot was already filled with tailgaters. "My dad spotted a shiny sedan moving through the lot," Frank told me, "and he said, 'Frank, follow me.' So dad and I followed the car until it stopped near an unmarked door of the stadium—and Lombardi stepped out.

"My dad approached him and said, 'Coach, I'm not sure if you remember me, but we met in Cleveland some years ago.'

"'Sure, Tony, I remember you,' Coach said. 'How're you doing?'

"'Well, Coach, my son and I drove from Cleveland to watch you win today.'

"They shook hands, and Lombardi said, 'I hope we don't disappoint you.'

"Dad introduced me to Coach Lombardi and we shook hands. Lombardi's hand was a vice, and I returned his strong grip. 'Your boy has a firm handshake,' Lombardi said. 'Do you play football, Frank?'

"'Yes, sir. I play for the Wildcats.'

"'What position do you play?'

"'All of them! I can run, pass, punt, catch, block, tackle, and kick like Lou Groza!' I told him that my teammates called me 'Frank the Tank,' then I asked him if he had any advice for a young person like me.

"Without hesitation, Lombardi said, 'Three things: First, choose to be a good leader. Leadership is about believing in yourself and making good choices. Second, surround yourself with the best people, like teachers and coaches, and be a good team player. Third, do everything your parents, teachers, and coaches ask you to do.'

"Then my dad said, 'Coach, don't you have to prepare for the game?'

"Lombardi said, 'No—we've been prepared since Friday. We're ready to go.' He seemed completely calm and confident. The Packers were fully prepared, and Coach Lombardi was all smiles. 'Where are your seats?' he asked.

"We told him our cousins had tickets for us in the upper deck. Coach said, 'Wait here.' Then he disappeared through the unmarked door. After a while, a man came out with an envelope containing four tickets—*right behind the Packers bench.*

"So we took our seats—best in the house—and as the Packers came out on the field, Coach Lombardi looked up at my dad and me, then he shouted to his players, 'You want to be like Frank the Tank!'

"The Packers won that day, 17 to nothing. And I came away with a lesson in leadership and preparation—nothing makes a leader more confident than being well prepared. Best of all, I came away with a memory of Vince Lombardi that has lasted a lifetime."

Vince Lombardi was a role model of the power of preparation. There is a famous quotation often attributed to him: "Luck is what happens when preparation meets opportunity." It sounds like something he would say, and it's definitely the way he lived and coached. But those memorable words actually came from the late, great Darrell Royal, longtime coach of the Texas Longhorns. I don't believe in "luck" myself, but I do believe that good things really do happen when preparation meets opportunity. If you make sure you're prepared for anything, then when your opportunity comes, you're going to have some amazing success.

When Vince Lombardi arrived to take over as head coach of the Green Bay Packers, he found a team that was woefully unprepared to win. Players were unmotivated, undisciplined, out of shape, and chronically late to practice. Lombardi knew he had his work cut out for him.

The first thing Lombardi did after accepting the job was go to church and spend several hours in prayer. Then he went home and started his preparation, spending several days with a 16mm projector and dozens of cans of game film. He ran the film backward and forward, and he studied each player in slow-motion and freeze-frame. He took meticulous notes on each player and charted plays on yellow legal pads. He made careful decisions about which players to keep and which to cut.

Lombardi realized he only had two players who were true standouts—offensive lineman Forrest Gregg and running back Paul Hornung. He saw little potential in his quarterbacks—at that point, Bart Starr was nothing like the legendary quarterback he would soon become under Lombardi's coaching.

In rebuilding his coaching staff, Lombardi wasn't looking for experience. Instead, he focused on hiring people who were passionate about winning and demonstrated good character. There were a few veterans on Lombardi staff, but most were young, untested rookies who came highly recommended. Coming seasons would prove that Lombardi chose well. He prepared his staff and his players to win.

Once he had his coaching staff in place, Lombardi began trading to strengthen his team. He rebuilt the Packers offense with players like running back Lew Carpenter from Cleveland, guard Fred "Fuzzy" Thurston from Baltimore, and quarterback Lamar McHan from the St. Louis Cardinals. (Lombardi selected McHan as the Packers starting quarterback for the 1959 season, but when McHan went out with a knee injury, Lombardi's second choice, Bart Starr, came in as a replacement and went on to a Hall of Fame career.)

One of the first phone calls Lombardi placed after joining the Packers organization was to running back Paul Hornung, the Packers Heisman-winning running back who had been selected first overall in the 1957 NFL draft. Amazingly versatile, Hornung could run the ball, pass it, receive it, and kick it. He was a hard-working, self-sacrificing, talented player who inspired his teammates—but after two years with the bottom-of-the-league Packers, he was discouraged to the point of quitting.

Lombardi told Hornung, "I've been looking at the films, and you're my left halfback." Hornung would later say that Lombardi's phone call "was the start of the eight best years of my life . . . Till he [Lombardi] got there, the whole place was so disorganized that, unless I'd been traded, I would've quit football in a year or two."[90] Under Lombardi's tutelage, Hornung became the emotional spark plug of the team and helped boost the Packers to greatness.

Having assembled his team, Lombardi began instilling a sense of pride into them. "You were chosen to be a Green Bay Packer," Lombardi said, and he let them know that being a Packer was going to be a mark of pride and tradition. Zeke Bratkowski told me, "Coach Lombardi required that we wear a coat and tie on the road, and that included the hotel lobby. He wanted us to think of ourselves as a team, even when we were not practicing or playing football. I think he was preparing us to be successful even after our football careers were over. Preparation was the key to Vince Lombardi's success. From training camp to the Super Bowl, he was meticulous about preparation."

Donald T. Phillips, in *Run to Win*, agreed that the purpose of the dress code was to prepare the Packers to build cohesion and unity on the team. "*Teamwork* was a prominent word in the vocabulary of Vince Lombardi as a head coach," Phillips said. "He wanted the Packers to think of themselves as a unit . . . [Lombardi said,] 'People who work together will win, whether it be against complex football defenses or the complex problems of modern society.'"[91]

Vince Lombardi believed in planning and preparation. Central to Lombardi's plan was the power sweep—which became known as the Packers Sweep. It was the simplest play in any coach's playbook. Yet through intense practice, Vince Lombardi used the Packers Sweep to dominate the NFL throughout the 1960s. He once told his team:

> Gentlemen, if we can make this play work, we can run the football. You think there's anything special about this sweep? Well, there isn't. It's as basic a play as there can be

in football. We simply do it over and over and over. There can never be enough emphasis on repetition. I want you to be able to run this sweep in your sleep. If we call the sweep twenty times, I'll expect it to work twenty times . . . not eighteen, not nineteen.[92]

Because of the Packers intense preparation, they executed the Sweep with near-flawless precision. Their opponents always knew it was coming, but they could do nothing to defend against it. The linebackers and defensive backs would watch the Packers line up in formation, and they'd start calling, "Sweep! Sweep!" But the defenders couldn't stop the Sweep. It was the Packers' bread-and-butter play—and the Packers were a hundred times better prepared to run it than their opponents were to stop it.

Wide receiver/tight end Gary Knafelc told me, "Vince Lombardi was a stickler for preparation. He never let anything to chance and was on top of every angle. That way he could handle any situation that came up. He told us there was no excuse for not being prepared, mentally and physically. He wanted us to work on our weaknesses to make them our strengths. His intense focus on preparation has helped me in every phase of my life, including my business pursuits."

Bob Hyland, who played guard for the Packers, told me that he believed Lombardi's West Point mentor, Red Blaik, deserves a lot of the credit for Lombardi's focus on preparation. "Lombardi was born to lead," he said, "but Red Blaik really helped to shape Lombardi's leadership style. Blaik gave him a master's degree in how to organize practices, analyze opponents, and prepare your players to win."

Roosevelt Grier played for the New York Giants from 1955 to 1962 and was a member of the Los Angeles Rams "Fearsome Foursome" from 1963 to 1966. He is also an actor, singer, and Christian minister. On June 5, 1968, Rosie Grier accompanied

Senator Robert F. Kennedy as his campaign entourage passed through the kitchen of the Ambassador Hotel. When a gunman leaped out and fatally shot the senator, it was Rosie Grier who subdued the shooter. Rosie became well acquainted with Coach Lombardi while playing defensive tackle with the Giants.

"Coach Lombardi was a stickler for organization and preparation," Grier told me. "He'd leave nothing to chance. His practices were intense. A lot of coaches will get after the rookie players and leave the star players alone but not Coach Lombardi. He'd yell at all of us equally. If we didn't perform in practice like he wanted, he'd line us up to scrimmage—and nobody wanted that to happen."

One of Rosie Grier's teammates with the Giants was Frank Gifford, who later went on to a long career in sportscasting. "I still feel Vince Lombardi's influence in my life today," Gifford told me. "Everything I've done in my career after my playing days, I credit to Lombardi. It comes down to two things: thorough preparation and working at a 110 percent level. Even now, in my early eighties, I still ask myself, 'What would Coach Lombardi do in this situation?' I'm still doing things the Lombardi way."

Packers defensive back Bobby Dillon agrees. "Vince Lombardi taught us to always be prepared because he was always prepared," Bobby told me. "Coach Lombardi would take no foolishness off of anybody. If you messed around during practice, Coach would make you pay for it. There was no joking around with him. Football was a serious business to Vince Lombardi, and he made sure we were serious about it, too."

Dale Hackbart was a defensive back with the Packers in 1960 and 1961. I asked him what he remembered most about Coach Lombardi. "His preparation," Hackbart replied. "As a leader, Vince Lombardi was always fundamentally prepared to play the next game.

He kept everything simple yet flexible, and he drilled us until we were as well prepared as he was. Nothing ever took him by surprise. When conditions changed, he made adjustments on the fly. He was prepared for anything and everything, including the unexpected."

COMPETENT TO MAKE DEMANDS

"When Lombardi said 'sit down,'" Forrest Gregg recalled, "we didn't look for a chair."[93]

Packers defensive end Willie Davis recalls that Coach Lombardi was demanding but fair, and his demands always focused on the pursuit of excellence in victory. One of the demands Coach Lombardi made on his players was punctuality—and he defined "punctuality" as being 15 minutes early. If you were on time, you were late. The requirement to arrive at least 15 minutes early was known as "Lombardi Time." Davis explained:

> If Coach Lombardi called a 5:00 p.m. meeting and the majority of the room was full at 4:45, he'd simply start the meeting, unaware he was starting early. Inevitably, we had players walking in with confused expressions on their faces . . . checking their watches to verify that they were still early. Regardless of the time, Coach Lombardi would stare them down or even say something. The message was clear: the meeting starts when Coach says it starts, and you better be here . . .

> I still show up at least fifteen minutes early for everything. I still judge myself, my actions, and even my habits, by how Coach Lombardi would have judged them. His influence is still that strong over me. I make sure that what

I'm doing with my life is helping me stay on the path to success, always, and I gauge that by what Coach Lombardi would have thought.[94]

Offensive tackle Steve Wright played four seasons with the Packers. He told me that living on Lombardi Time became a lifelong habit for him as well. "I still run my life on Lombardi Time," he said. "If you arrive ten or fifteen minutes early, you're on time—barely. If you arrive on time, you're late for sure. It's been fifty years since I first met Vince Lombardi, and I still arrive early to all my appointments. Coach Lombardi drilled it into me, and it stuck."

Art McNally, the former director of officiating for the NFL, used to visit the NFL training camps at the start of every season to go over the rules and rule changes with the players and coaches. "One year," McNally told me, "I went to Green Bay for a session with the Packers. I had set it up for 2 p.m., so I arrived early to put some things up on the blackboard. Well, I *thought* I was early, but I wasn't. I was shocked to see the meeting room already filled up. At 1:45, Vince Lombardi walked in and said, 'Art, let's go.'

"After the session, I went over to Bart Starr and said, 'I'm so sorry I got here late. I hate being late.' Bart said, 'You're not late. We're always fifteen minutes early. That's how we operate. We're on Lombardi Time.' Pretty soon, the entire officiating team adopted Lombardi Time. To this day, that's how the NFL refs operate. If they're to leave the hotel at 10 a.m. for the stadium, they're all ready to go and waiting in the hotel lobby at 9:45. That says something about Lombardi's influence."

Vince Lombardi earned the right to demand the utmost from his players because he demanded nothing less from himself. I interviewed Matt Henrikson, West Point class of 1950, who played center for Army under Red Blaik and assistant coach Vince Lombardi.

Henrikson told me, "Vince Lombardi was steady and consistent and always fixed on his objectives. He expected excellent performances from all of us, but he understood that we would make errors. His mission was to correct those errors. Vince Lombardi was a young coach, and we could see him working hard to learn from Coach Blaik. He developed his coaching competence very rapidly."

I asked Henrikson what impressed him most about Coach Lombardi. "He was a hands-on coach who would actually get down and scrimmage with us," Henrikson told me. "He demanded a lot from us—but he demanded just as much from himself. I was a linebacker and a long snapper. One day in practice, Coach Lombardi was working with me. He pushed me and banged me around. Then he said, sort of apologetically, 'I don't have the strength I had when I played at Fordham.' Well, I was glad he didn't, because he beat me up pretty good that day."

Frank Gifford was one of the last of the 60-minute players, playing both offense and defense even after platoon football became commonplace in the NFL. Gifford shared with me a rare personal glimpse of Vince Lombardi. "The Giants had a disastrous season in 1953 under head coach Steve Owens," he told me. "Owens was fired and replaced by Jim Lee Howell, who turned over most of his coaching duties to his two top assistants, Vince Lombardi, who joined the organization in 1954, and Tom Landry. Lombardi was a very intelligent guy, and very disciplined. He expected as much from himself as he did from us. He was always looking for ways to grow and improve himself as a coach.

"The Giants roster was filled with military veterans who had been in combat in World War II and Korea. These guys had been in actual shooting wars, and they didn't take coaching as well as the younger guys who were fresh out of college. It was a challenge for the coaches to get the veterans to listen to them.

"One day, Vince Lombardi called me into his office. My first thought was, *Oh no, they traded me.* But that wasn't the case. I was amazed because he wanted my advice. He said, 'What am I doing wrong?'

"There I was, twenty-four or twenty-five years old, and Coach Lombardi was asking me for advice. I said, 'You're ordering these veteran players around like children. You won't gain their respect and cooperation that way.' I wasn't sure how he was going to take it, but he asked so I told him. He thought about it for a few moments, then he thanked me.

"Everything got better after that. He was always listening, learning, and trying to improve himself as a coach. Not many coaches would ask advice from their players, but Coach Lombardi was special that way. He really wanted to be the best coach he could possibly be. The way he expected so much from himself, the way he was so eager to learn was a huge factor in his greatness as a coach in the NFL.

"When Vince Lombardi left the Giants to coach the Packers, I knew he was going to be a great head coach. Paul Hornung called me and asked, 'What kind of coach is Vince Lombardi?' I said, 'Paul, get ready to run. He'll run your tail off.'"

Wide receiver Pat Richter was a first-round pick of the Washington Redskins in the 1963 NFL draft, and he went on to play eight seasons in Washington. He told me, "When Vince Lombardi came to Washington from Green Bay, we all knew his reputation for promptness, discipline, and toughness. But he also commanded instant respect. Vince Lombardi had a great way of doing things. Much of it was due to his efficiency during our practices. He spent half as much time at practice as George Allen did, and he got twice as much done."

I asked Pat Richter if Coach Lombardi had made a long-term impact on his life. "Oh, absolutely," Richter said. "Vince Lombardi was coaching life as well as football. He kept driving us to practice professionalism. He wanted us to be on the same page at all times. His great quote was, 'You can't have a careless attitude or this enterprise will not be successful.' I've thought of those words many times since, and Coach Lombardi's principles have guided many of my decisions over the years. He was telling us that, after our NFL careers, we needed to act with professionalism toward our work, our financial responsibilities, our families, and everything else in life. He wanted us to know that, though we were committed to winning as a team, what we did with our lives after football was far more important than winning or losing a football game. He wanted us to be successful as human beings, not just as football players."

Coach Lombardi's players were constantly amazed at his competence in so many aspects of his jobs as coach and general manager. Linebacker Dave Robinson told me, "Vince Lombardi did everything well. Anyone would have his hands full just being head coach of the Packers, but he was coach and general manager, and I don't know how he did it all. He coached us, ran the draft, made the trades, negotiated the contracts—and he rarely made a mistake. He had an uncanny knack for doing what was right."

Lombardi was attentive to all the details that, taken together, resulted in excellence. Royce Boyles, who has authored several books on Packers history, told me, "As the general manager, Vince Lombardi was on top of every little thing about the franchise. He had the parking lots marked according to his specifications. The field was striped just so. The restrooms were cleaned to his demanding standards. Nothing escaped his supervision. Everything had to be excellent. Nothing less would do."

Donny Anderson, who played halfback for the Packers, told me that Lombardi earned the right to be demanding. "Coach Lombardi told us that if we did things his way, we would be winners," Anderson said. "And when we did things his way, we won, just like he promised. That inspired confidence. We were ready to follow him anywhere. He was a disciplinarian and he was very demanding. He had a military attitude, probably from his coaching experience at West Point. But he did what he said he'd do. He molded us into a cohesive team. We played as a unit, not as individuals. Coach Lombardi kept his word. He turned us into winners."

Boyd Dowler joined the Packers in 1959. "I was a rookie football player," Boyd told me, "and Vince Lombardi was a rookie head coach. I had been signed as a quarterback, and Coach Lombardi brought in all his quarterbacks in June. There were six of us in the room. (Coach later decided to make me a flanker, and that turned out to be a great fit for me.) At that first meeting, I couldn't help but be impressed. I thought, 'This guy means business and I'd better do what he's asking.' Lombardi was demanding but not unreasonable. I played every game Vince Lombardi coached at Green Bay and his intensity never changed. He coached every practice, every game, at full throttle."

EXPERIENCE PRODUCES COMPETENCE

History has shown Vince Lombardi to be one of the most competent leaders in any field. Yet, when he arrived in Green Bay, no one had any idea how amazingly well qualified he was for that position. The truth is, hardly anyone believed in Vince Lombardi but

Lombardi himself. His leadership competence had been forged and tempered over his coaching career, from St. Cecilia to Fordham to West Point to the Giants. But his ability to take complete charge and achieve great results had never been tested at the pro level.

The Vince Lombardi who arrived in Green Bay in 1959 was largely an unknown quantity. He was, in fact, the Packers' second choice as head coach. The Green Bay organization's first choice, Iowa's Rose Bowl-winning head coach Forest "Evy" Evashevski, had turned down the job, apparently thinking the Packers were unsalvageable. Compared to the highly regarded Evashevski, the unknown Lombardi was viewed as a placeholder until someone better came along. Sure, he had a lot of experience as an assistant, but he had no track record as a head coach. Expectations were low.

A lot of coaches might have turned down the offer to coach in Green Bay. What if the team was simply beyond redemption? If Lombardi failed in Green Bay, he might never get another chance to prove himself. But Lombardi believed in his ability to turn the Packers around. When Green Bay offered him the job, he pounced on it. He saw the challenge of revitalizing the moribund Packers as a golden opportunity to demonstrate his leadership competence. In fact, what better way to prove himself than to take the worst team in the league and make it the best?

Of course, there must have been a little voice nagging at Lombardi, saying, "But what if you can't pull it off?" I'm sure Lombardi must have pondered that question several times a day after he arrived in Green Bay. But if he felt any lingering doubts, he didn't show it. Vince Lombardi exuded nothing but confidence—and an air of confidence conveys an aura of competence.

Where did Vince Lombardi gain the competence and confidence to be a great leader? For the most part, it came from experience.

Vince Lombardi paid his dues.

Though Lombardi gained fame as a football coach, some of his most important early coaching experience came as a basketball coach at tiny St. Cecilia High School in Englewood, New Jersey. Basketball was not Lombardi's game. In order to coach the boys' and girls' basketball teams, he first had to teach himself the game by reading books, then attending and observing college games at Madison Square Garden. Though self-taught as a basketball coach, he amassed an impressive record over eight seasons at St. Cecilia, leaving with 105 wins and 57 losses. In 1945, he coached the Saints to the only state basketball championship in the school's history.

One of the strangest incidents in Coach Lombardi's coaching career occurred when his St. Cecilia boys' basketball team hosted Bogota High, February 29, 1940. Lombardi's Saints were having an off season and were out of the running for the postseason tournament. Bogota High, from a small town near Hackensack, had already devastated St. Cecilia earlier in the season and was tournament bound. The Bogota coach wanted to conserve his team's strength for the tournament a few days later.

The game began, and the Saints put up the first shot, which bounced off the rim. The Bogota center grabbed the rebound—and stopped. Now, this was in the era before such rules as "three in the key" and backcourt violations. In those days, players could simply stand and hold the ball, refusing to advance to the forecourt without any penalty being called. And that's exactly what the Bogota team did.

Once Coach Lombardi realized what the opposing coach had in mind, he was furious. Lombardi ordered his players to back off and wait for Bogota to show some offense. For several minutes, the Bogota center stood as motionless as a stone Buddha, staring impassively. The people in the stands began to jeer and boo. The standoff continued, and Lombardi let it play out to the end of the quarter. The second quarter played out the same way.

At the start of the second half, St. Cecilia won the tipoff, and a Saints player attempted a shot from the outside. No good. The Bogota center again got the rebound—and again he froze in place.

Tom "Red" Cosgrove, one of the players who was there that night, recalled, "It was hard to watch. It was a circus, but you couldn't do anything about it." With the score tied at zero at the end of the third quarter, the crowd's displeasure was deafening. The standoff dragged on into the fourth quarter. Finally, with just minutes left to play, Lombardi shouted to his players, "Go get 'em!"—and the Saints sprang into action.

Another of Lombardi's players, Mickey Corcoran, said, "We pressed, grabbed the ball and scored." The Saints were filled with pent-up frustration and anger over the Bogota ball-hogging. Their opponents, however, seemed dispirited and demotivated by their coach's "game plan" of just standing around, doing nothing. The result: The Saints were ready to play, Bogota was not. Lombardi's players scored three goals from the floor, while Bogota scored only a single point from the free-throw line. Final score, St. Cecilia 6, Bogota 1.

The moment the final buzzer sounded, Lombardi stormed across the court and confronted the Bogota coach, nose to nose, accusing him of cowardice and disgracing the game. Though no blows were struck, officials separated the two coaches. Lombardi did not have a civil word for the Bogota coach for years afterward.[95]

That game was a learning experience for young Coach Lombardi. Sometimes your opponent will throw a strategy at you that is so bizarre, you may not know at first what to do. If Lombardi told his players to go after the ball, they might run themselves ragged in an extended game of Keep-Away. But Lombardi adjusted quickly to the new situation, pulled his players back, and refused to play the opponent's game. He waited them out. Then, in the final minutes, he told his team to unleash their fury against their flat-footed opponent—and it worked. It was a lesson in "thinking outside the box"—the kind of thinking that enabled him to outwit many opponents over his career.

In his high school and college coaching career, Vince Lombardi learned many lessons that increased his competence and deepened his leadership wisdom. Longtime NFL executive Ernie Accorsi shared with me a story about how Coach Lombardi learned to mellow out and set a better example of self-control. Ernie told me, "I had a dear friend, Larry Ennis, who coached high school football in New Jersey. He also worked on Red Blaik's coaching staff at West Point, beginning in 1950.

"One day at practice, Larry saw Vince Lombardi going crazy with his players, jumping up and down, screaming and hollering. Coach Blaik signaled to the young man who was filming the practice, making sure the cameramen kept filming Lombardi's antics.

"After practice, the coaching staff gathered to study film. All of a sudden, up pops that piece of film with Vince Lombardi carrying on that day. Back and forth the film goes and Lombardi is sweating bullets. Then Blaik said, 'Coach Lombardi, just what were you teaching our young cadets during today's practice?' Ennis told me, 'I never saw Vince Lombardi react like that again.'"

Jack Martin, who was a running back for Army from 1948 to 1950, had a good term to describe Coach Lombardi's tendency to bellow and shout at his players: "over-exuberant." He told me, "At West Point, Vince Lombardi was a young assistant coach, a new coach. So he was walking in soft shoes just like his players. He was full of vigor and emotion. Colonel Blaik considered him over-exuberant. Lombardi led loudly, a lot of shouting at the players, and Colonel Blaik would caution him not to treat the cadets that way. Lombardi's leadership style was just growing when he got to West Point. I think he learned how to coach and lead under Colonel Blaik."

David Maraniss, in *When Pride Still Mattered*, suggests that the reason Vince Lombardi liked coaching was that it was a substitute priesthood. The deeply religious Lombardi had once planned to enter the priesthood, where he could be a father figure and a leader—someone who helps to build character and point young lives in the right direction. One advantage coaching had over the priesthood, Maraniss wrote, was that "the coaching profession did not force him to repress his emotions." A coach could blow off steam at his players without shocking anyone—after all, coaches were expected to be loud and emotional. Priests were expected to be soft-spoken and devotional. Lombardi chose the right path.

Vince Lombardi's early experiences as an assistant coach prepared him well to be the head coach of the Green Bay Packers and Washington Redskins. By paying his dues and by being mentored by coaches like Red Blaik, Lombardi gained valuable experience that magnified his competence.

COMPETENCE PRODUCES RESPECT

Vince Lombardi earned respect by giving respect. Speaking on behalf of officiating crews, Art McNally told me, "Vince Lombardi commanded tremendous respect among the referees. He'd holler at you but never in a way that was personally insulting or demeaning. I never heard him use profanity."

Now, that statement struck me. Coach Lombardi had a widespread reputation for being profane when he was angry. Yet Lombardi never cussed at Art McNally and the other officials. He yelled, he argued, he tried to get the refs to see things his way—but he was never insulting, never abusive. Loud, yes. Angry, yes. But in his own way, Coach Lombardi showed respect for the authority of the officiating crew. That's why Art McNally never heard the blue language that Lombardi's players heard on a regular basis. On the team, Lombardi was the authority figure. On the field, Lombardi respected the authority of the officials.

Competent leadership generates respect—not only from your players but even from your opponents. John Madden told me that one of the great honors of his career was coaching against Lombardi. As defensive coach of the Oakland Raiders, Madden helped get the Raiders to Super Bowl II at the Miami Orange Bowl, where they suffered a 33-14 defeat at the hands of Lombardi's Packers.

"That was the last game Vince Lombardi coached with the Green Bay Packers," Madden told me. "My biggest thrill of that event was when I looked across the field and stared at Vince Lombardi on the sidelines. I thought, 'Holy cow, I'm coaching against Vince Lombardi! I'm on this side of the field and Lombardi's on that side, and I'm telling my linebackers how to stop Vince Lombardi's offense. Unbelievable!' There I was, a young guy thirty years old, matching wits with the great Vince Lombardi in the ultimate game of the year. The man was my idol. How many guys get a chance to go up against someone they respect that much, in the biggest arena of all?"

Author Royce Boyles told me about the respect the Packers had for their coach. "Vince Lombardi didn't do a lot of coaching during the games," Boyles told me. "One night, deep into their retirement, a group of Lombardi's Packers were sitting around a table at a res-

VINCE LOMBARDI ON LEADERSHIP

taurant in Wisconsin. Boyd Dowler made this observation: 'I don't think Vince Lombardi called ten plays in the entire nine years he coached us in Green Bay.' Dowler was in awe of Coach Lombardi's intense preparation for each game. In practice, Lombardi was able to prepare his players so thoroughly that they knew exactly what they needed to do on game day. The Packers would have a light practice on Friday afternoon, and at that point Lombardi's work was done for the week. His players had an enormous respect for the way Coach Lombardi prepared them to be winners."

Longtime Newark sportswriter Jerry Izenberg also told me about the respect the old Packers had for their coach. "Some of Lombardi's players hated him, because he was so tough—but none of them ever doubted him. They all respected him and believed in him. I covered the first Super Bowl when Green Bay played the Kansas City Chiefs. The Packers seemed awfully cocky about the whole event, so I said to Fuzzy Thurston, 'Why are you so sure you're going to beat a great team like Kansas City?' Fuzzy grinned and said, 'We'll win the game because we have the best coach in football.' He meant it. He believed it."

Well, of course he believed it. Lombardi was the best in the game.

The Fifth Side of Leadership is competence. Leaders of great competence build organizations that compete to win. They make sound plans, prepare their followers, and build confidence. That's why Vince Lombardi was a leader of championship teams.

CHAPTER 6

THE BOLDNESS OF VINCE LOMBARDI

A man can be as great as he wants to be. If you believe in yourself and have the courage, the determination, the dedication, the competitive drive, and if you are willing to sacrifice the little things in life and pay the price for the things that are worthwhile, it can be done.
—**Vince Lombardi**

It's called the "fair catch kick," and it may be the least-used play in the NFL rulebook. The rule states: "After a fair catch, the receiving team has the option to put the ball in play by a snap or a fair catch kick (a field goal attempt), with fair catch lines established ten yards apart." That last phrase means that the defending team has to stay ten yards from the kicking team's line of scrimmage—the defenders cannot rush the kicker.

Few football fans even know this rule is in the book, and fewer still have ever seen it attempted. The reason the fair catch kick is so rare is that the catching team almost always elects to run plays from the line of scrimmage in an attempt to score a touchdown. After all, fair catches are generally not made in field-goal range, and there's little point in attempting a 70-yard field goal.

But on September 13, 1964, at Green Bay's City Stadium (now Lambeau Field), the Packers squared off against the Chicago Bears—and Vince Lombardi probed the dark, cobwebby corners of the rulebook and came up with the fair catch kick. Near the end of the first half, Chicago punted the ball away. Packers halfback Elijah Pitts signaled for a fair catch and hauled in the ball at the Packers' 48-yard line.

There were still a few seconds on the clock, and more than 42,000 people in the stadium that day—fans, media, officials, and players of both teams—assumed the Packers would take a knee, then head for the locker room. Only one person in that stadium thought differently: Vince Lombardi. He walked over to referee Norm Schachter and informed him that the Packers would attempt a fair catch kick on the final play of the half.

The fans looked on, completely mystified, as the Packers lined up with quarterback Bart Starr placeholding the ball on the line of scrimmage. Halfback and placekicker Paul Hornung booted the ball out of Starr's hold—and it sailed through the uprights. That 52-yarder added three points to the Packers lead.

In the end, those three points didn't materially affect the outcome of the game, since the Packers won 23 to 12. At the post-game press conference, a reporter asked Lombardi if he and the team had worked on that play in practice. Coach Lombardi laughed and replied, "We've never worked on it in our lives! We almost faked ourselves out!" Moreover, the chances of anyone ever seeing that play again in this lifetime, Lombardi added, "are nil."

In that prediction, Lombardi was mistaken. Four years later, in 1968, the Chicago Bears pulled a switcheroo and called for a fair catch kick against the Packers at Lambeau Field. That kick, too, was successful and it sealed a 13-10 Bears victory. By that time, Lombardi was still general manager but no longer head coach of the Packers.[96]

Dusting off a never-used play from the forgotten corner of the rulebook was a bold move by a bold leader. It's one of the reasons Vince Lombardi exemplified the Sixth Side of Leadership—Boldness.

TAKING RISKS—AND TAKING RESPONSIBILITY

Boldness is the willingness to seize timely opportunities, to dare to do the unexpected, to act firmly and decisively without looking back. Bold leaders take reasonable, calculated risks in order to achieve important goals. Boldness doesn't mean being reckless or throwing caution to the wind. Rather, it means committing yourself to a course of action, withstanding hardship and opposition, and accepting the possibility of failure in order to achieve great success.

You cannot be a leader without the Sixth Side of Leadership. A leader must be bold and courageous. There's a reason you never hear the phrase "timid leadership"—it would make no sense, it's a contradiction in terms. A leader who masters his or her fears and projects an air of confidence will embolden the entire organization.

Bold decisions don't always result in victory, and great leaders must accept the consequences of their decisions. To be sure, Coach Lombardi made some bad decisions, and he was the first to admit it. But bad decisions often make excellent learning experiences, and Vince Lombardi always learned the lessons of his mistakes. Once he learned a lesson, he never repeated the mistake.

Take, for example, the NFL Championship game against the Philadelphia Eagles at Philly's Franklin Field on December 26, 1960. That was Coach Lombardi's first, last, and only postseason loss as coach of the Green Bay Packers. And yes, he made some bold decisions in that game—and he later regretted those decisions.

On the Eagles' first offensive play of the game, Packers defensive end Bill Quinlan intercepted a pass thrown by Norm Van Brocklin. The Eagles were off to a disastrous start—a turnover giving the Packers the ball at the Eagles' 14-yard line. The Packers gained eight yards on the next three running plays, setting up a fourth-and-two on the Eagles 5-yard line. Lombardi decided to go for it with a run play. Bart Starr took the snap, handed off to Jim Taylor—but Taylor was stuffed short of a first down. The Packers came away empty handed.

In the third quarter, the Packers again faced a fourth-and-short situation, this time at the Eagles' 25-yard line. Lombardi called another running play. Déjà vu—Jim Taylor was stopped short again. Twice the Packers had been within easy field goal range, but Lombardi had gambled on touchdowns—and lost both times.

In the end, the Packers fell to the Eagles, 17 to 13. Lombardi took the blame for the loss, citing those two fourth-down gambles as the deciding factors. The Packers had out-rushed the Eagles 223 yards to 99, had gotten 22 first downs to Philadelphia's 13, and had run 77 plays to the Eagles 48. Replace those two fourth-down attempts with two field goals, and the Packers would have won the NFL title. It was a painful lesson that Lombardi never forgot.

After the game, Lombardi told sportscaster Ray Scott, "I learned my lesson today. When you get down there, come out with something."[97] Lombardi obeyed that lesson throughout the rest of his career. I'm not saying Lombardi never again gambled on fourth-and-short. He still took bold risks whenever the odds and the stakes made the gamble worthwhile. But he made every effort, once he got that close to the goal line, to finish the drive and put points on the board.

Bold leaders like Vince Lombardi are willing to take a calculated risk—and willing to accept the blame when the gamble fails. Bold leaders also learn the lessons of failure and adjust future plans accordingly. Boldness does not mean recklessness. Boldness means taking reasonable risks for the sake of important goals.

LEADERSHIP IS NOT A POPULARITY CONTEST

Bold leaders need to be respected, but they don't need to be liked. Many people fail in their leadership roles because they have a neurotic need to have everybody like them. Wanting to be liked by your followers will make you timid and hesitant in situations where you need to be bold.

In all the interviews I had with people who knew and played for Vince Lombardi, not one of them described him as a tyrant. Yes, he was tough. Yes, he could scream and shout profanity. Yes, he often made his players hate him at the time. But every player I interviewed, without exception, spoke of Coach Lombardi with respect—and, yes, with affection. In spite of his harsh demeanor—or maybe because of it—this coach, who didn't care whether or not his players liked him, ended up being not only liked but loved.

Leadership is not a popularity contest. Bold leaders must make tough decisions—decisions that will make a leader about as popular as a root canal. One of the toughest jobs a bold leader must do is discipline his or her people. A leader has to be tough enough to enforce the rules, but not be so rigid and harsh as to lose respect. It's a balancing act, and Coach Lombardi maintained his balance remarkably well.

Sportswriter Jerry Izenberg told me a story that illustrates Coach Lombardi's approach to team discipline. "Willie Davis once told me, 'You were scared to challenge Coach Lombardi and too smart to disobey him.' But I remember one time in Lombardi's first year as coach when one of the Packers disobeyed him. Coach Lombardi had a strict rule: No wives allowed in training camp, period. A talented rookie running back named Alex Hawkins showed up at training camp with his wife. She was almost nine months pregnant. I guess Hawkins thought Lombardi would make an exception in the case of a wife who is about to have a baby. Hawkins thought wrong. Lombardi exploded and let Hawkins have it for violating his rules. Then he calmed down and told Hawkins his wife could stay with Marie at the Lombardi's home until the baby arrived. But Alex Hawkins was forbidden to go over to see her.

"One day before practice, Vince Lombardi announced to the squad that Alex Hawkins was the father of a baby boy and he would be allowed to go to the hospital to visit his wife and newborn son. Was Lombardi going soft? Not a chance. Right after that announcement, Vince Lombardi traded Hawkins to Baltimore, where he ended up having a good career. But that trade sent a message to the team: Lombardi was saying, loud and clear: 'I won't have anyone on this squad who won't obey my rules.'"

Another disciplinary issue that tested Coach Lombardi's wisdom was the Paul Hornung suspension. Hornung was one of the elite running backs in the history of the game. On April 17, 1963, NFL commissioner Pete Rozelle suspended both Hornung and a standout Detroit Lions defensive tackle, Alex Karras. Their crime: betting on NFL games.

Hornung didn't try to defend or minimize his actions. Mobbed by reporters as he was coming off the golf course, Hornung responded to the news of his suspension with instant contrition. Choking back tears, he said, "I made a terrible mistake. I realize that now. I am truly sorry. What else is there to say?"

Coach Lombardi had very little warning about the suspension—and he was unhappy about being blindsided by the news. He called Hornung by phone and said, "You should've told me—I think I could have rectified it."

Hornung didn't argue with his coach—he knew better. He listened and he said, "Yes, sir," to everything Lombardi said.

As they talked, Lombardi appealed to the fact that Hornung, like himself, had been raised in the Catholic Church. Lombardi told him, "You stay at the foot of the cross . . . Keep your nose clean, and I'll do my best to get you back. But, mister, stay at the foot of the cross."

Lombardi wasn't just angry with Hornung. He felt deeply disappointed and personally wounded—not just about the gambling but because Hornung didn't come to him when he learned he was in trouble with the league. Lombardi was so discouraged and personally devastated over this one incident that he confided to Marie, Commissioner Rozelle, and other close friends that he wanted to resign as the Packers head coach. It took the encouragement of all of them to convince him to stay.

Hornung was barred from playing the entire 1963 season. Then, on March 16, 1964, the NFL reinstated both Paul Hornung and Alex Karras. Hornung, eager to please his coach and show his contrition, called Lombardi and offered to begin workouts at the Packer training facility in early May, two months ahead of training camp.

Coach Lombardi, as tough as ever, would not go easy on Hornung. "Mid-April would be better."[98]

Paul Hornung ultimately put the scandal and the suspension behind him. He went on to play three more stellar seasons with the Packers and retired only after a pinched nerve in his neck made it impossible to play. He was inducted into the Hall of Fame in 1986.

WHERE DOES BOLD LEADERSHIP COME FROM?

One of the boldest decisions Coach Lombardi ever made was to cede most of the on-field decision-making to the guys in the trenches. He knew that it would be a disaster to micromanage decision-making from the sidelines. So one of his chief goals as the coach of the Green Bay Packers was to empower his players to think on their feet and make good decisions under pressure. He designed his plays to have plenty of options, so that his players could make split-second adjustments to changing conditions.

Lombardi mentored Bart Starr and empowered him to do most of his own play-calling. He put Ray Nitschke in charge of directing the defense. The entire design of the Packers Sweep was to give maximum flexibility and decision-ability to his players so that they could be nimble and responsive on the run. In this way, Coach Lombardi reserved overall strategic decision-making powers to himself, while distributing tactical decision-making authority to his assistants and players.

On May 8, 1967, Fordham University presented Vince Lombardi with the Insignis Medal, honoring him not only as a great coach but also as a great teacher. The featured speaker was Lombardi's old boss at West Point, Coach Red Blaik, who knew Lombardi well. Blaik provided an apt character sketch of his former assistant, including these words:

> He is a demanding fundamentalist, intolerant of those who fail to meet their own potential. But he is also a tireless teacher who respects the intellect . . .

He is motivated to success—to win, if you will—not for personal glory but rather for the personal satisfaction that comes from great accomplishment . . .

He is fearless and of great candor, but he also knows it takes a special emotional and mental drive to overcome the personal fallibility that one knows who must make the great decision.[99]

Some leaders seem to have been *born* bold. But I believe most leaders need to acquire the mind-set of a bold leader.

Decision-making is the essence of leadership. Therefore, one of the key traits of a complete leader is the ability to be boldly decisive. The failure to make a timely decision can be more costly than making a bad decision. Great leaders can't afford to be timid, hesitant, or indecisive.

Great leaders don't punt the responsibility for decision-making to a committee. Leaders decide. A failure to decide is a bigger mistake than any wrong decision you might make. A wrong decision can be corrected, but there's no way to correct indecision. Whatever you do, don't dither—*decide.*

Leaders accept full responsibility for their decisions. That's the kind of leader Vince Lombardi was. His bold, decisive style of leadership was the result of a combination of key ingredients, including:

- *Experience and training,* which provides a leader with the knowledge base to make good decisions. Vince Lombardi gained a wealth of experience, training, and mentoring as an assistant coach at Fordham, West Point, and the New York Giants. Even his experiences coaching basketball and football at the high school level at St. Cecilia helped prepare him for the role of a lifetime as an NFL head coach.

- *Wisdom*, made up of sound judgment and sound principles that guide a leader in making moral decisions. Vince Lombardi learned the principles of moral leadership from his Jesuit instructors and especially from his mentor and confessor at St. Cecilia, the school's athletic director, Father Tim Moore. In fact, Father Tim was a close friend, spiritual guide, and confidant throughout Coach Lombardi's career and remained close to Lombardi right up until his death.

- *Confidence*, which comes from amassing a record of successes. As a leader makes more and more decisions that turn out well, that leader learns to trust his or her own judgment and make decisions quickly, without costly hesitation and second-guessing. Coach Lombardi learned over the years to be self-confident without becoming overconfident.

- *Intuition*, an indefinable but vital ability to make high-quality decisions "from the gut," based on incomplete information. Coach Lombardi often made decisions about people, strategy, and career opportunities relying primarily on his intuition. He had an inner "guidance system" that served him well throughout his career, and it helped him to make bold, wise decisions.

As we examine Coach Lombardi's life, a number of key principles emerge: If you believe you're on the right path, stay on it. Never yield to criticism and opposition—persevere. If you lead boldly and decide firmly, you may not always be popular, but odds are, you'll ultimately be respected. Continually seek out bigger and more daunting leadership challenges. Every time you conquer a tough challenge, your confidence level ratchets up. Every step Vince Lombardi took in his career was a step up to a tougher challenge. Meeting each challenge and overcoming each obstacle helped to prepare him to become the greatest football coach of all time.

Are you growing in your leadership skills? Are you taking on every new leadership challenge that comes your way? If you can honestly answer yes, then you are learning to lead the Lombardi Way.

The life of Coach Lombardi proves that bold leadership must be built on a foundation of moral principles. A leader who has a sturdy framework of values and principles has a built-in guide to sound decision-making. When your values and principles are clear, your range of options becomes more sharply defined. You'll know that certain options are off the table because they don't conform to your values and principles. The best options become obvious because they align with what you believe to be true and morally sound. Principled decisions tend to be high-quality decisions.

Decisions not rooted in sound principles are often based on all the wrong considerations: Which decision will make me more popular? Will it benefit me in the short term? Which decision requires the lowest risk and least inconvenience to me personally? If those are the considerations that drive your decision-making, you're not a leader of principle.

But when your most important decisions align with your guiding principles, you can be confident you're doing the right thing. Every decision you make will be firm, final, and confident. At the end of each day, you'll hit the sack and sleep well, knowing you did your level best as a leader—and you'll have no worries or regrets.

So lead like Lombardi. Let your boldness be your leadership trademark. Set bold goals and pursue them with bold confidence.

BOLD IN THE COLD

I first met Bart Starr in 1967, when I was running the Phillies farm club in Spartanburg, South Carolina. As one of our summer promotions, we brought Bart to the ballpark for a personal appearance. We paid him $500—top dollar for a personal appearance in those days. Bart spent the entire day with us—speaking at a luncheon, signing autographs, playing golf with our boosters, and throwing out the first pitch in the game. Bart could not have been more gracious. (I also brought Paul Hornung to Spartanburg for a promotional appearance in 1967, the year after he retired; Paul was equally gracious to our fans, and I'm proud to have known both of these Packers legends, Bart Starr and Paul Hornung, for nearly 50 years.)

Becoming acquainted with Bart Starr during the summer of 1967 made it all the more meaningful, later that year, to watch him play in the most infamous game in football history—the 1967 NFL Championship game, better known as the Ice Bowl. It was played on New Year's Eve, 1967, at Lambeau Field. That game had everything: blood-freezing sub-zero weather, high stakes (the winner would go on to Super Bowl II), and an intense coaching rivalry (Vince Lombardi's Packers versus Tom Landry's Dallas Cowboys), plus a dramatic finish. In fact, the game came down to a single bold decision on a final play as time was running out.

Weather forecasts had predicted that game day would be cold, around 20 degrees Fahrenheit with clear skies—but the forecasts were wrong. At the 1 p.m. kickoff, the temperature on the field was *beyond* cold—minus 15 degrees with an average wind chill of about minus 48 degrees. A system of heating coils under the turf had malfunctioned, rendering Lambeau field more of a hockey rink than a football field. The officiating crew could not blow their whistles without pulling the skin from their lips. They were forced to use voice commands to make calls. CBS sportscaster Frank Gifford offered this terse commentary on the weather: "I'm going to take a bite of my coffee."[100]

Cowboys head coach Tom Landry recalled, "We stayed in a motel in Green Bay, where the doors opened to the outside. I remember going to bed and getting up for breakfast in the morning, and I couldn't believe it. Everything was ice. It was like the North Pole. I think we were in shock most of the game."[101]

But Packers tackle Bob Skoronski expressed his team's perspective on the weather: "We dealt with the weather like it wasn't even there. The game of football, as we were told by our boss, was made to be played in any kind of condition. It wasn't played necessarily on a dry field, a wet field, or a no-grass field. It's played wherever it's played, so don't be worried about the weather. Everybody contends with it, both you and your enemy."[102]

Mary Jane Van Duyse Sorgel told me how she and her Golden Girls cheerleading squad braved the bitter weather of the Ice Bowl. "The Ice Bowl was really something. It was unbelievably cold. When I tried to twirl my baton, it was like trying to twirl an icicle. We had ten more girls than usual for that game, because NBC wanted us to hold signs, one letter for each girl. They were spelling out 'Happy New Year from NBC,' that sort of thing.

"We wore extra stockings, but it wasn't nearly enough. Yet the girls were committed to performing, even under those conditions. One girl even had frostbitten toes. But even though they were suffering, none of the girls wanted to leave until the game was over.

They bundled up and huddled together on the sidelines until the final play."

Bart Starr and the Packers faced Don Meredith and the Cowboys. The game was played in short-yardage passes and slippery sprints across a field that might as well have been a concrete parking lot in Siberia. By halftime, the Packers led 14-10. The third quarter was scoreless. In the fourth quarter, the Cowboys scored a touchdown and took a 17-14 lead.

With 4:50 remaining, Bart Starr led the Packers' final drive, starting at his own 32-yard line. Managing the clock with precision, he steadily advanced the ball with a series of handoffs and short slant passes. Reaching the Cowboys' 1-yard line, the Packers' drive stalled. Twice, Bart Starr handed off to running back Donny Anderson, and both times, Anderson slipped on the ice and fell at the line of scrimmage. On third and goal, with 16 seconds remaining, Starr burned his last timeout and went to the sidelines to talk to Coach Lombardi.

Now, I can't prove it, but I have a suspicion that as Bart Starr was walking toward the sidelines, Coach Lombardi was thinking back seven years to the championship game against the Philadelphia Eagles. In that game, Lombardi had *twice* told his Packers to go for it on fourth down—and both times, the Packers came up empty. He had made bold decisions—and later regretted them.

Lombardi knew what the prudent decision should be in this situation. Coaching wisdom dictates that if you face a stronger opponent in such situations, it's usually best to roll the dice and go for it on fourth down. But if your team is the stronger team, it makes more sense to play it safe, send out the kicking team, and leverage your team's superior strength to win the game in overtime. The Packers had led throughout most of the game and had statistically outclassed the Cowboys in first downs, total yards, passing yards, and completions. Logic—plus the lessons of that playoff game in 1960—dictated that Lombardi send in the field-goal unit and put the game into sudden death overtime.

But it quickly became apparent that Vince Lombardi had other plans. The Packers offense stayed on the field while Bart Starr conferred with his coach.

Up in the broadcast booth, CBS broadcaster Pat Summerall told his crew to watch for a rollout pass—only an incomplete pass would give the Packers time for a fourth-down attempt. With no timeouts remaining, a failed running play would permit time to run out—and the Packers would lose, 17 to 14.

On the sidelines, Bart Starr told Coach Lombardi that his running backs were finding it impossible to get traction—they kept slipping on the ice. But the offensive linemen were able to hold their footing. Starr suggested a daring play: let the lineman wedge an opening, and Starr would keep the ball and break into the end zone.

Lombardi didn't hesitate. "Run it," he replied, "and let's get the hell out of here." It was a bold decision—sheer audacity. Lombardi was betting the entire 1967 season on one play.

Starr went out to the huddle and called "Brown right 31 Wedge." Then the Packers lined up and Starr called the signals. Center Ken Bowman snapped the ball, then he and Jerry Kramer double-teamed left defensive tackle Jethro Pugh, opening a hole. Bart Starr ran for daylight and plunged into the Promised Land.

So much was riding on that one play. If Bart Starr had failed to score, it's safe to say that Vince Lombardi would not now be remembered as the figure of legend he has become. An NFL official once said, "No other team but Vince Lombardi's Packers could have driven sixty-eight yards under those conditions against the best defense in the NFL. They didn't make a single mistake—not a fumble, not a penalty, not one botched play. They executed perfectly."[103] And Forrest Gregg told me, "I don't think the Packers' execution of that drive, in those conditions, can ever be surpassed."

Everyone watching the game that day expected Vince Lombardi to take the safest course. Instead, he took the *boldest* course—and won the game. And that's why the Ice Bowl is considered one of the greatest football games of all time.

After the game, the press corps asked Coach Lombardi to explain his decision. Lombardi replied, "We went for a touchdown instead of a field goal because I didn't want all those freezing people up in the stands to have to sit through a sudden death. If you can't run the ball in there in a moment of crisis like that, then, mister, you don't deserve to win. Those decisions don't come from the mind. They come from the gut."[104]

The Packers had it all that day: The touchdown. The win. The league championship. A trip to Super Bowl II.

Sometimes, logic says, "Play it safe." But there are times when a leader's gut says, "Seize the opportunity. Take the risk."

Royce Boyles shared a fascinating insight with me about Vince Lombardi's Ice Bowl decision. Royce draws a parallel between the Ice Bowl and the 1958 NFL Championship Game between the New York Giants and the Baltimore Colts. In 1958, Lombardi was the offensive coach of the Giants; Tom Landry ran the defense. Late in the game, facing fourth-and-inches in their own territory, the Giants called a timeout. Lombardi, Landry, and head coach Jim Lee Howell conferred on the sidelines.

"Lombardi lobbied Jim Lee Howell," Royce told me. "He argued for the bolder course and said, 'Any great team can make a yard.' But Landry took the opposite view. He said, 'The smart thing to do is to punt the ball away. Our defense will hold them and we'll win the game.' Howell listened to Landry and the Giants punted it away — but the defense didn't hold them as Landry had promised. Johnny Unitas led the Colts in one of the most famous drives in football history — and the Colts won in overtime.

"Now, fast-forward to the Ice Bowl. Here are the same two coaches, Lombardi and Landry, only now they are opposing each other as head coaches. And there's Landry, 'the thinking man's coach,' the finesse guy, and he's expecting a rollout. Even after working alongside Lombardi with the Giants, he didn't expect the bold, blood-and-guts, run-it-down-your-throat play-calling that was Lombardi's stock-in-trade. How appropriate is it that the play Bart Starr suggested, the play Lombardi okayed, was fundamental blocking and tackling—Lombardi's trademark."

The bolder course is usually the best course. One of the most dangerous things any leader can do is "play it safe." To lead like Vince Lombardi, be bold. When the moment of opportunity comes, seize it and turn it to your advantage.

That's the path of greatness.

CHAPTER 7

THE SERVING HEART OF VINCE LOMBARDI

Football is like life—it requires perseverance, self-denial, hard work, sacrifice, dedication, and respect for authority.
—Vince Lombardi

When you picture Coach Vince Lombardi putting his Packers through the infamous nutcracker drills at the practice facility, yelling and even cussing at them, it's hard to imagine that he once coached girls' basketball at tiny St. Cecilia High School. It's true—the legendary Vince Lombardi once coached a team of girls dressed in blue bloomers and stockings, playing in front of "crowds" of a few dozen parents and siblings.

Rosemary Maroldi Diemar played forward on the St. Cecilia girls' team in 1942. She remembers Coach Lombardi as a demanding task master—"He had us doing layups until my legs used to want to fall off"—and as a caring mentor who made the girls on the team feel valued. "I was small," she recalled, "but he would say, 'That's okay because you're fast.' In those days, girls' basketball wasn't important, but Mr. Lombardi never acted like we weren't important."

Clearly, Lombardi didn't treat his lady basketballers as harshly as he treated the Packers—yet he still found ways to inspire and motivate those girls to play hard and win. Rosemary Diemar recalls, "I don't remember losing a game with Mr. Lombardi. It never occurred to us that we could lose for him; he wouldn't stand for it. It was unthinkable. We wanted to win for him."

She recalled that, as a coach, Lombardi was a positive and encouraging motivator: "If he said, 'Good shot,' I was ecstatic. If he had to correct or criticize us, it was never in a way that you resented. When we finished the season, he gave us all gold basketballs to wear on a chain around our necks."[105]

(Royce Boyles told me that Lombardi continued this tradition into the Packers era. He gave gold football bracelet charms to the ladies in the Packers organization—one gold charm for each championship, set with a precious stone. After each of the first four championships, he gave a charm with an emerald—a green stone symbolizing the Green Bay Packers. After Lombardi's fifth and final championship in Green Bay, he gave them a gold charm with the diamond. In *The Lombardi Legacy*, Royce included a photo of the charm bracelet Lombardi gave to his administrative assistant, Lori Keck.)

Many people have an impression of Vince Lombardi as a screaming, butt-kicking intimidating coach—and yes, he could certainly be all of that and more. But people fail to realize that much of that screaming was calculated for effect. Lombardi wasn't a raging madman—though sometimes it served his purposes for his players to think he was. His assistants would often see him go off in a tirade on his players—then he'd turn around and flash a big satisfied grin that the players couldn't see. Appearing to be out of control was part of his deliberate plan for *maintaining* control.

Gale Gillingham understudied and succeeded veteran left guard Fuzzy Thurston and played his entire ten-season career (1966–1974, 1976) with the Packers. Royce Boyles shared Gillingham's recollections with me (which first appeared in Royce's book *The Lombardi Impact*). Recalling Coach Lombardi's seemingly unprovoked tirades during training camp meetings at St. Norbert College, Gillingham concluded that Lombardi's ranting and raving was calculated for effect. "[Lombardi] must have rehearsed some of that stuff. He would find reasons to be completely upset about something. There were times he was just unbelievable. He would come completely unglued. I think everybody suffered the same under him and that made us all pull together."

Vince Lombardi, the master psychologist, used a seesaw, push-me-pull-you method of tearing his players down psychologically, then building them up again. And I should add that I *don't* recommend you try this at home or in your leadership role. Lombardi made an intense study of what motivates players to perform, plus he made an intense study of each of his individual players. As Lombardi once said, "There are other coaches who know more about X's and O's, but I've got an edge. I know more about football players than they do."[106]

But even after all the time and effort he invested in understanding what motivated each one of his players, there were a few times when he went too far. If you are a leader in a corporation or a church or a school, and you try to use Lombardi's intense motivational methods on your own people, you'll probably find yourself going to sensitivity training at best and possibly the unemployment office. These are different times, and they call for a different approach.

I know there are coaches who rant and rave and abuse their players like galley slaves—and then they justify their brutal behavior by saying, "Hey, if it was good enough for Lombardi—!" Any leader who thinks Vince Lombardi got results simply by screaming at people has completely misunderstood the man—and doesn't know the first thing about leadership. If you have the first six sides of leadership but you don't have the Seventh Side: A Serving Heart, then you don't have leadership, period. You're just bossing people around.

One coach who failed to understand this principle was George Wilson, coach of the Miami Dolphins expansion team from the 1966 through 1969 seasons. Prior to taking the job in Miami, Wilson had coached some good Detroit Lions teams from 1957 through 1964. In fact, Wilsons's Lions went 11-3 in 1962 and handed Lombardi's Packers their only loss that season—but Lombardi won the title. Though Detroit was in the same division as Green Bay, and Wilson's teams faced off against Lombardi's Packers many times, Wilson's view of Lombardi's coaching style was undoubtedly tainted by Leonard Shecter's *Esquire* piece, which portrayed Lombardi as a bullying maniac.

"I'm tired of all this Lombardi business," Wilson complained. "Everyone makes him out to be such a great coach. Given the same material, I'll beat him every time. I can get a team up on the day of a game. I bawl guys out as much as Lombardi does, but I don't holler at a fellow in front of his teammates. I don't want to embarrass him. That's just a big show, and I'm not going to do it."[107]

Wilson didn't understand. Lombardi's approach to coaching was never about bawling guys out, either in front of their teammates or in private. Yes, Lombardi was tough and his methods could be harsh—but at the base of everything Lombardi did was a foundation of love and a serving heart.

The same year Wilson made that statement, his Dolphins finished 3-10-1—and Wilson was fired. His replacement, former Baltimore Colts head coach Don Shula, took the same core group of players that Wilson had worked with, and coached them to a 10-4 record in 1970, 10-3-1 in 1971, and a 14-0 undefeated regular season in 1972, plus back-to-back NFL championships in Super Bowls VII and VIII. (Shula's coaching style has often been compared to Lombardi's.)

Royce Boyles told me a story that highlights the stark contrasts between George Wilson's leadership style and Vince Lombardi's. On October 7, 1962, the Lions and Packers met at City Stadium (now Lambeau Field) in Green Bay—the last two teams still undefeated. The Packers trailed the Lions throughout the game, and in the final minute, the Lions led 7-6, had possession of the ball at midfield, and were chewing up the clock by keeping the ball on the ground. The Packers seemed powerless to stop them.

Then, inexplicably, Lions quarterback Milt Plum gambled by throwing a pass. Intended receiver Terry Barr slipped and fell—and Plum's ill-conceived pass fell into the hands of Packers defender Herb Adderley, who returned the ball 40 yards to the Lions' 22-yard line. With 33 seconds left to play, the Lions defense went onto the field knowing the game was lost. As Lions defensive tackle Alex Karras passed Milt Plum on the field, he unleashed a volley of obscenities at his team's quarterback. Seconds later, Paul Hornung kicked a field goal to defeat the Lions, 9-7.

Royce Boyles concluded, "There were some years that George Wilson had the second-best team in football. But it was his misfortune to be in the same division as Vince Lombardi. Who won the big games? Who won the games that mattered in order to advance out of the division? It wasn't George Wilson. His Detroit Lions did manage to beat the Packers in a rematch on Thanksgiving Day, handing Green Bay its only loss of the 1962 season—but Lombardi's Packers won the title that year.

"Milt Plum's bone-headed last-second interception didn't just cost the Lions one game. It nearly tore the team apart. When the game was over, Alex Karras stormed into the locker room and fired his helmet at Plum. He had every reason to blame Plum, who would have won the game if he had just stayed focused on eating up the clock.

"The Packers were a reflection of their coach—totally disciplined and focused on winning until the clock ran out. And Milt Plum seemed to be a reflection of George Wilson—a coach who ran his mouth but didn't finish the job."

Anyone who thinks successful coaching—or successful leadership in any arena—is about intimidating people or bawling them out doesn't understand the key to Vince Lombardi's leadership greatness. It wasn't Lombardi's bullhorn voice or the bulging veins in his neck that made him a great leader. It was his serving heart. Coach Lombardi himself put it this way: "I believe everybody wants discipline, especially young people. But one has to be careful of the spirit in which it's given. They'll take it if it's done in the spirit of teaching . . . even of love, like the discipline one gets from a mother and father."[108]

Vince Lombardi was a genuine *servant* to his players. He loved them, and they respected him and loved him in return.

WHAT DO WE MEAN BY "LOVE"?

Former Chrysler CEO Lee Iacocca writes in his autobiography about a dinner conversation he once had with Vince Lombardi. Iacocca asked Lombardi about his formula for building a winning team. Lombardi replied that there were three essential ingredients for building a winning team, whether a sports team or a business team.

First, Lombardi said, you have to teach your players the fundamentals, the essential principles of the game. Next, you have to maintain discipline on the team so that they function together as a unit, not as a collection of individuals. Third, you have to instill a sense of mutual love into the team.

"If you're going to play together as a team," Lombardi explained, "you've got to care for one another. You've got to *love* each other. Each player has to be thinking about the next guy and saying to himself: 'If I don't block that man, Paul [Hornung] is going to get his legs broken. I have to do my job well in order that he can do his.' The difference between mediocrity and greatness is the feeling these guys have for each other. Most people call it team spirit. When the players are imbued with that special feeling, you know you've got yourself a winning team."[109]

The kind of love Lombardi spoke of needs a bit of explanation. *Love* is a word that is misused all the time in our culture. As C. S. Lewis observed in *The Four Loves*, the ancient Greeks used four different words for our word *love*. The Greeks had a word for romantic love, a word for friendship love, a word for parent–child love, and a word for love that is unconditional, a love that is not a feeling but a deliberate choice. That fourth kind of love, unconditional love, is what the ancient Greeks called *agape* (pronounced *uh-GAW-pay*). And that is the kind of love Vince Lombardi described to Lee Iacocca, the kind of love he sought to build among his players.

Unconditional love is essential to teamwork. When you put a group of players together, you hope they will bond into a tight-knit group of friends. But that doesn't always happen. Sometimes there is friction among players. Personalities clash. For one reason or another, some teammates just don't like each other.

But the kind of love Vince Lombardi tried to build among his players can pervade a team even when some players don't like each other. Believe it or not, players who don't like each other can *love* each other—if they learn teamwork love, unconditional love. When loving your teammates is a choice, not an emotion, you can *choose* to tolerate, accept, support, encourage, forgive, and celebrate with people you don't really like. You can be teammates with people you'd never be friends with. As Lombardi himself said, "It's the team! Teamwork is what the Green Bay Packers were all about. They didn't do it for the individual glory. They did it because they loved one another."[110]

Now, because that word *love* has so many different connotations in our culture, Lombardi's use of that word sometimes provoked confusion and even ridicule from sportswriters. I don't think he ever regretted using that term in the locker room, but he did regret using it when talking to the media. He once said, "Every year I try to think of a new word for it"—referring to Packer spirit, that special sense of unity and cohesion that the Packers had. "Last winter at the Super Bowl, I called it something I have been sorry about ever since. When those tough sportswriters asked me what made the Packers click, I said, 'Love.' It was the kind that means loyalty, teamwork, respecting the dignity of another—heart power, not hate power."[111]

You can't have teamwork without unconditional love. In fact, it's usually the unlikable people who need love the most. As Lombardi once said, "I don't necessarily have to like my associates, but as a man I must love them." Without unconditional teamwork love, you and your team won't get very far. But if you as a leader can love all your players unconditionally, and if you can teach unconditional love to your entire team or organization, then you may win a championship or two. Don't take my word for it—just ask Bart Starr. He once said,

"This type of love for each other probably best explains the fact that we won five NFL championships in seven years."[112]

Packers defensive end Willie Davis told me, "Vince Lombardi was the only coach I ever had who told us that we should love each other as teammates. Some coaches would talk about teamwork and pulling together and supporting each other, but Coach Lombardi called it *love*. He absolutely wanted us to love each other. I was the defensive captain, so it was my job to speak with my teammates and make sure that everyone was practicing the principles the coach laid out. I can assure you that 99 percent of the players on that team adhered to what Vince Lombardi was saying.

"There was love on that team. That's what made the Packers special. Everything we accomplished in Green Bay was built on that love. Coach told us that if we lived out that kind of love for each other, we would become a great football team. The results speak for themselves. And I'm not just talking about what we accomplished on the field. The love we had for each other in the Green Bay Packers has carried on long after our playing days have ended, and we are still close friends to this day."

Teamwork, like love, is really a form of servanthood. It involves submerging your own ego for the sake of serving and lifting up your teammates, so that you can all win together. Coach Lombardi taught and exemplified the servanthood ethic of unconditional love and teamwork. Packers backup quarterback Zeke Bratkowski told me a story that illustrates the serving heart of Coach Lombardi.

"One day, I went out to play golf. I got home that night and realized that my Super Bowl ring had fallen out of my pocket. I was panic-stricken and couldn't sleep all night. The next morning, Coach Lombardi came over and asked about my ring. I told him I couldn't find it and I was sick about it. Then he reached in his pocket and handed it to me. I had never told him about losing the ring, but somehow, he had found out about it. He had gone out on the golf course the previous night with a flashlight, and he had found the ring. How many coaches would do that for a player? I'll never forget that."

How many leaders have a serving heart like Vince Lombardi? Do you?

A TEAM BUILT ON LOVE

The Packers struggled through the 1960 season and suffered a tough 23-10 loss at the Thanksgiving Day game in Detroit. There was very little holiday cheer as the Packers boarded the plane for the trip back to Green Bay. Coach Lombardi had said very little to them after the game, and some undoubtedly wondered when he was going to lower the boom for the mistakes they had made—a punt blocked for a safety, plus two fumbles.

But when Vince Lombardi boarded the plane, he astonished his players by being all smiles. He invited them to have not one but *two* beers on him during the flight home. Then he stood in the aisle and gave his players a pep talk about the changes they were going to make so that they could win the rest of their schedule.

Arriving back in Green Bay, Lombardi treated all of his players and their families to a Thanksgiving dinner with all the trimmings at the Elks Club downtown. He had the projector brought over from the training facility, and instead of game film, he screened continuous cartoons for the kiddies in a room downstairs. During dinner, he went from table to table, chatting with the players and their wives, letting them know that he valued them and they were *family*. More than a genial host, Vince Lombardi was a *servant* to his players that evening. As tackle Bob Skoronski later recalled, Lombardi was the "father figure for the whole group."[113]

In my interviews with players going back to Lombardi's days as an assistant coach at Fordham and West Point, I learned that Coach Lombardi took an interest in his players' families long before he became head coach of the Packers. Andy Lukac played for three years at Fordham University under then-assistant Coach Lombardi, 1948–1950. Andy told me, "After Vince Lombardi left Fordham and became an assistant coach at West Point, he and I kept in touch from time to time. When my bride and I sent him a wedding announcement at the Point, he wrote back and wished me luck. He enclosed two tickets to the Army–Navy game."

And Packers linebacker Dave Robinson told me, "Vince Lombardi was the first coach to give the players' wives a gift—a mink stole, a color television set, a silver tea service—after winning a championship. Some of the other NFL owners were upset by this idea—they didn't like the precedent it set, so they complained to the league office. Commissioner Pete Rozelle called Vince Lombardi and tried to rein in his generosity. Lombardi said, 'Pete, you run the NFL and I'll run the Packers.' Rozelle tried to change Lombardi's mind, but no such luck. Finally, Rozelle gave up and said, 'All right, go ahead and give the gifts to the wives, but please keep it quiet—don't announce it publicly.' Lombardi agreed to do that."

Bill Anderson joined the Green Bay Packers in 1965, after playing most of his career for the Redskins. Though he only played two seasons under Coach Lombardi, they were spectacular seasons, and he earned an NFL championship ring in Super Bowl I. He went on to a three-decade-long career as a broadcaster with Tennessee football.

"Vince Lombardi was a player's coach. He was tough, but he cared. I had only been in Green Bay a month when my dad passed away. I tried to get a commercial flight to North Carolina for the funeral, but there were none available. Coach Lombardi came to me and said, 'Get ready to go. I've got a private plane and a pilot to get you there.' He had paid for everything I needed to get from Green Bay to Hendersonville on time. He told me, 'The pilot will wait for you. Just come back whenever you feel ready.' When Vince Lombardi told you something, you could count on it. He was a straight shooter. That's why guys wanted to play for him, and that's why we'd do anything to win for him."

Wide receiver Bob Long told me, "Vince Lombardi always emphasized 'the team, the team.' He never appeared in a team photo. He felt that a team photo was for the players, not the coaches. He rarely shook hands with his players, because he didn't want to show any preference or favoritism. Other teams had all those nicknames—Purple People Eaters, Steel Curtain, Fearsome Foursome—but Vince Lombardi never allowed nicknames about how good the Packers were."

A few years ago, I had Forrest Gregg on my local radio show in Orlando. Coach Lombardi had once called him the "best player I ever coached." I told Forrest that I'd heard there was a great sense of family and love among the Lombardi-Era Packers, and I asked him if those reports were true.

"Oh yes," Gregg said, "it was true then, and it's still true today. We're all in touch with each other and we care about each other. I bought a home in Colorado Springs, and my old teammate Willie Davis bought a home in the same neighborhood. We hang out together. All of us old Packers from the Lombardi days still get together. Bart Starr, Paul Hornung, Jimmy Taylor, Boyd Dowler,

Carroll Dale—we're all in touch with each other. Our families get together all the time. Coach Lombardi built the team on love, and the love goes on. Nothing will ever stop that."

Vince Lombardi was even a servant to strangers. As I was working on this book with Advantage Publishing, I learned that the director of publishing, Patti Boysen, had a Vince Lombardi story to share with me. "One time, my father was in New York on business," she said. "It was a cold, rainy night, and he was on the sidewalk in front of his hotel, trying without success to flag a cab. A black limo pulled up at the curb right in front of him. The window rolled down and a man in the back of the limo asked if he could give my father a ride.

"Dad accepted the offer and climbed into the limo. As he sat next to the man and they started talking, my father realized who it was: Coach Vince Lombardi. He was going out to dinner and asked if my father wanted to join him. My father accepted the invitation and had one of the most memorable evenings of his life as the dinner guest of Vince Lombardi."

STEPPING DOWN FROM THE PRIESTHOOD

As we saw earlier, a coaching career appealed to Vince Lombardi because it was, in many ways, like a calling to the priesthood. Lombardi was a father figure to his players, and some of his inspirational speeches were practically homilies, liberally sprinkled with quotes from the Scriptures. It's hardly surprising, then, that Vince Lombardi spoke to his players about a Christian concept like unconditional love. It's also hardly surprising that Coach Lombardi wanted his Packers to become more than great football players—he wanted them to become great human beings. He wanted them to become successful in the biggest game of all—this game called Life.

In the 1966 NFL Championship Game, Packers safety Tom Brown ended a Cowboys comeback drive with an interception in the end zone. That interception sealed the win and sent the Packers to Super Bowl I. I interviewed Tom Brown, and he told me, "Coach Lombardi wasn't just a coach. He was a teacher and mentor. He was continually teaching us life lessons, many of which had little to do with football but everything to do with being effective in the game of Life. I can still hear his voice in my thoughts, and I still remember the principles he drilled into us. I've talked to a lot of my old teammates over the years, and we all agree that not a day goes by that we don't think about Vince Lombardi and how he helped to structure our lives."

We can see Coach Lombardi's focus on influencing and inspiring his players through the words he spoke. He once told them, "After the cheers have died down and the stadium is empty, after the headlines have been written and after you are back in the quiet of your own room and the championship ring has been placed on the dresser and all the pomp and fanfare have faded, the enduring thing that is left is the dedication to doing with our lives the very best we can to make the world a better place in which to live."[114]

In February 1968, Vince Lombardi stepped down as head coach of the Packers. He handed off the head-coaching job to his assistant, Phil Bengtson, and stayed on as general manager. It was not a hasty decision. He had thought about it all through the 1967 season. Initially, Lombardi said that the intense time commitment of working both jobs—head coach and general manager—was too much for him. The long days, the long nights, and working seven days a week from July through January had taken its toll. Lombardi spent so much time away from home that, after a long practice, he would sometimes head home and drive past his house without recognizing it.

But the time commitment wasn't why he gave up coaching. As Lombardi explained to *Sports Illustrated*, the *real* reason he stopped coaching was that the burden of winning had become too great. "The pressures were so horrible," he said. "The pressure of losing is bad—awful . . . but the pressure of winning is worse—infinitely worse, because it keeps on torturing you and torturing you. At Green Bay, I was winning one championship after another. I couldn't take it because I blamed myself after every loss. I felt I'd let them down. You know, if we'd just won every other title, or if we'd lost to Dallas in '66 or '67, I'd still be in Green Bay. Forever."[115]

When Lombardi handed off the head-coaching job to his assistant, he said, "Under his leadership and under his direction, Green Bay football will continue to be excellent. Green Bay football will continue to grow."[116] But without Vince Lombardi, Green Bay football didn't continue to be excellent. In their first season without Lombardi as head coach, the Packers finished with a losing record and missed the playoffs.

For the first time in his career, Vince Lombardi found himself watching the Packers games from a luxury box in the sky instead of from the sidelines. And he hated it. During the 1968 season, Lombardi confided to friends that giving up coaching had been "a horrible mistake." Word got around that Lombardi might be willing to return to coaching.

In January 1969, Lombardi resigned as general manager of the Packers and accepted an offer from the Washington Redskins: in exchange for a $100,000 annual salary and $500,000 worth of Redskins stock, he would once again be both head coach and general manager of an NFL franchise. Lombardi rejected the notion that he was motivated by money. "I don't need the money," Lombardi retorted. "Money I've got. I need to *coach*."[117]

Lombardi knew that coaching was his calling, his priesthood, his ministry, his mission. He had been coaching all his adult life—at the high school level, the college level, and in the NFL. He had given up coaching for a year—and instantly knew it was a mistake. He hadn't just stepped down from a *job*. He had given up a huge piece of his *identity*. All his life he had been teaching, mentoring, and shaping young lives—and he had lost sight of how important coaching was to his character and makeup.

When Lombardi returned to coaching, he was like a wayward priest rediscovering his faith and returning to the priesthood—*his* version of the priesthood, which he practiced in the locker room and the stadium. For a year, he had lost himself. Now he was going back where he belonged. Vince Lombardi was a servant. Coaching was his way of serving others.

In his formative years, Lombardi had been instructed by the Jesuits—the Society of Jesus—and the example of Jesus, the Leader who served, was deeply imprinted in his soul. He had undoubtedly heard many times the words of Jesus—"I am among you as one who serves" (Luke 22:27). When Vince Lombardi returned to coaching, he returned to serving.

"GENTLEMEN, LET'S BE WINNERS"

Soon after Lombardi's arrival in Washington, a reporter asked him why he chose Washington from among all the offers he received. Lombardi replied, "Because it is the capital of the world. And I have some plans to make it the football capital."[118]

One of Lombardi's priorities was to meet with his new quarterback, Sonny Jurgensen. Both coach and quarterback had heard many stories about each other, and it was important that they size each other up and build a trusting relationship.

Before their first meeting, Jurgensen called his pal, Paul Hornung of the Packers, and asked if all the stories of Lombardi the Tyrant were true. Hornung laughed and said, "Sonny, you're gonna love the guy."

When I interviewed Sonny Jurgensen about his time with Coach Lombardi, he told me about their first encounter. "I'll never forget that first meeting. I was a little nervous about our new coach, but he put me at ease right away. He said, 'Sonny, don't try to emulate anyone else. Don't try to be someone you're not. Just be yourself.' That was great advice. He also said I would have to be the leader, I would have to set the example."

Lombardi went on to explain his philosophy of the offense and the quarterback position. By the end of that meeting, Jurgensen said, he was wishing the season would begin the very next day.

At the Redskins summer training camp in Carlisle, Pennsylvania, on July 10, 1969, Lombardi assembled his players and addressed them for the first time. "Gentlemen," he said, "I have never been with a loser, and I do not think I'm ready to start at this time in my career. You are here to play the game of football, and I am here to see that you play it as well as your abilities will allow . . . I am going to push you and push you and push you because I get paid to win and so do you . . . Gentlemen, let's be winners."[119]

Lombardi quickly established his familiar routines and rules. The coaching staff found out about Lombardi Time, and the assistant coaches put the word out to the players. The Redskins had not had a winning season in 14 years and had finished the previous season with a 5-9 record. Lombardi knew he would need to invest a lot of prayer in this season if he was going to turn things around.

One of Lombardi's first stops in Washington was the Cathedral of St. Matthew the Apostle on Rhode Island Avenue. He knocked on the door and introduced himself to the parish priest, then asked when the first daily Mass was scheduled.

"At 7:30 a.m.," the priest replied.

"Why don't you change it to 7:00?" Lombardi said. "It would fit my schedule better."

The coach was clearly used to getting his way—but the priest at St. Matthews was no pushover. Mass would begin at 7:30.[120]

On the Redskins first day of practice with their new coach, Lombardi watched his quarterback, Sonny Jurgensen, go through his paces. After a while, Lombardi stopped the practice and took Jurgensen aside. "You're throwing the ball too quickly," he said.

Jurgensen, who had been playing with the Redskins since 1964, said, "Coach, I have to get rid of it quickly because I'll get hit. We don't have the best offensive line here."

"Don't worry about it," Lombardi assured him. "We'll give you the best protection you've ever had."[121]

As Lombardi prepared for the season ahead, Marie worried about him. During Lombardi's final year in Green Bay, he had suffered bouts of weakness and dizziness. After their arrival in Washington, he experienced a severe inflammation of the prostate. Yet his return to coaching seemed to revive and invigorate him. He told Marie he was excited about the season ahead, and it felt great to be coaching again.

One of the first tests of Lombardi's serving heart came in the form of a running back from the University of Idaho, the Redskins' first pick in the 1967 draft, 6-foot-4 Ray McDonald. His first two seasons with the team had been disappointing—but McDonald's performance on the field was not the only problem. Ray McDonald was gay, and the coaches and players all knew it. McDonald had been arrested by D.C. police in 1968 for a tryst in a public park, so his sexual orientation was no secret—and some of the coaches and players were uncomfortable about it.[122]

Coach Lombardi's son, Vince Jr., told *USA Today* that his father gave specific instructions to his coaching staff. He said, "My dad told the Redskins assistants on that 1969 team when it came to Ray McDonald, 'Don't you hold his manhood against him—coach him up to be the best player he can be.'" This didn't mean the coaches were to go easy on McDonald. Lombardi wanted them to push him the same way they pushed the other players—but they should never disparage him because of his sexual orientation.

This was right around the same time as the Stonewall riots in Greenwich Village that led to the gay rights movement. Clearly, Vince Lombardi was ahead of American society in his concern for the feelings of this homosexual player. Vince Jr. explained, "My dad's brother Harold was gay, so that's why my dad was very open and accepting."[123] And Coach Lombardi's daughter, Susan Taylor, said, "My father was way ahead of his time. He was discriminated against as a dark-skinned Italian American when he was younger, when he felt he was passed up for coaching jobs that he deserved. He felt the pain of discrimination, so he raised his family to accept everybody, no matter what color they were or whatever their sexual orientation was."[124]

The Redskins players were not used to the relentless Lombardi coaching style. They thought Lombardi's practices were like being fed to a meat grinder. But one of Coach Lombardi's old Packers—defensive back Tom Brown—was traded to the Redskins the same year Lombardi took over as head coach. Brown could tell that Coach

Lombardi was not the same. "To me he was not as aggressive," Brown recalled. "I figured, well, he's just trying to feel his way around. But maybe he didn't have the energy, the enthusiasm, to do what he did in Green Bay."

At the same time, Lombardi quietly confided to a few friends that he was feeling tired—and he was wondering if he had made the right decision by returning to coaching. Though Lombardi's health was declining, he enjoyed the D.C. scene. He quickly made friends in high places, including *Washington Post* editor Ben Bradlee, humorist Art Buchwald, and Ethel Kennedy, widow of Senator Robert F. Kennedy, who had been assassinated in June 1968.

Ethel had been in seclusion since her husband's death but came out to see Lombardi's Redskins defeat the New York Giants 20-14 at Robert F. Kennedy Stadium. She attended a victory celebration that evening in the Lombardi home and later sent Lombardi a thank you note, saying, "You realize it isn't Sonny's arm but Marie's Hail Marys that pull us through every Sunday." Ethel Kennedy later credited Vince and Marie Lombardi for easing her out of mourning and back into Washington social life.[125]

The Redskins finished the 1969 season with a record of 7–5–2, the Redskins' first winning season since 1955. It's interesting to note that Lombardi's first season as the Packers' head coach produced almost an identical record, 7-5 (the two-game difference is because 1959 was a twelve-game season and 1969 was a fourteen-game season).

Lombardi had promised his quarterback that he was going to get better protection from the offensive line—and he delivered on that promise. As a result, Sonny Jurgensen completed 65 percent of his passes that year. "That season with Coach Lombardi," Jurgensen told me, "was an incredible experience. I was looking forward to more seasons under his coaching. It was tragic, just tragic the way we lost him. I was sad for his family, of course, but I was also sad for us as players. I have spent eighteen seasons in the NFL, and that one amazing year with Vince Lombardi was my favorite. I didn't want it to end."

Sportscaster Paul Kennedy was a 16-year-old high school student in Washington, D.C., during Lombardi's only season with the Redskins. One spring morning in 1970, Paul and his friend Dave Hunzicker were sitting in a breakfast spot on K Street, reading the menu, when two men in business suits entered the establishment. Paul instantly recognized one of the two men—it was Coach Vince Lombardi, stopping by with a colleague after his customary morning Mass.

Paul and Dave, both avid Lombardi fans, decided to have a little fun. Raising their voices just loud enough to be annoying, they began poking fun at the Redskins. Lombardi must have known he was being baited. He turned and smiled at the two mischievous teens, saying, "Aren't you boys supposed to be in school?"

The boys explained that they had the day off from school. Lombardi asked some more questions, sizing them up. They talked for a few minutes about school and football, then the boys asked Lombardi for his autograph.

"Sure," Lombardi said, taking pen and paper and signing his name for the boys. "Listen, my office is right across the street. Stop by and I'll show you around."

After breakfast, the boys went across the street to the Redskins office. When a security guard tried to shoo them away, Lombardi appeared and said, "Let them in. They're friends of mine."

Then Lombardi proceeded to give the two young fans a tour of the offices. He introduced them to future-Hall of Fame wide receiver Bobby Mitchell, who happened to be in the building that day. Lombardi told the boys stories, pointed out pictures on the wall, and was very generous with his time.

Finally, a secretary walked up and interrupted. "Coach, you have an appointment," she said.

"I've got to go," Lombardi said. "Stay around if you like. It was nice meeting you."

That was in the spring of 1970. That summer, Coach Lombardi was diagnosed with cancer. By September, he would be gone. After he died, the *Washington Post* printed his picture in full color on the front page. Paul Kennedy clipped that portrait from the newspaper and framed it alongside Lombardi's autograph. Paul showed me that framed photo and signature, and he told me, "I see Vince nearly every day."

Vince Lombardi gave an incredible gift to young Paul Kennedy and his friend Dave Hunzicker. He gave the gift of his time, the gift of his gracious personality, the gift of his serving heart. There was nothing those two boys could ever do to repay Coach Lombardi for his kindness. And he didn't want to be repaid. He just wanted to serve.

Serving is what real leaders do.

DEATH OF A SERVANT

In June 1970, while preparing to coach his second season with the Redskins, Lombardi took sick. He was admitted to Georgetown University Hospital for tests related to digestive tract problems he'd been ignoring for more than two years. Doctors discovered he had a fast-growing cancer—an aggressive anaplastic carcinoma—in his lower colon. After an exploratory surgery in July, his doctors concluded that the cancer was terminal.

After the announcement of Lombardi's illness, President Nixon called him and told him the entire nation was praying and rooting for him. Lombardi vowed to keep battling the cancer. Many of Coach Lombardi's former players, fearing they might never see him again, made the pilgrimage to his hospital room from all around the country.

Sportswriter Jerry Izenberg told me, "Vince Promuto was a guard with the Redskins from 1960 to 1970. He had trouble keeping Coach Lombardi's rules. Every player learned right away that you don't break Lombardi's rules—so, during the 1969 season, there was tension between Promuto and the coach. Well, Promuto told me that when Vince Lombardi was in the hospital, dying of colon cancer, he and Sonny Jurgensen sneaked into Coach's hospital room. Promuto told me he walked over to Lombardi's bedside and held his hand and said, 'Coach, I thank God He sent you to be my coach.' That was the impact Coach Lombardi had on Promuto, on all his players. He changed their lives."

In September 1970, Willie Davis was a member of the TV broadcast crew, working at a Giants–Chargers preseason game in San Diego. Giants' owner Wellington Mara took Davis aside and told him that Lombardi's health was far graver than had been publicly announced. If Davis wanted to see his old coach again, he had better go soon. Davis knew Lombardi was sick—but this was the first he'd heard how serious it was.

Immediately after the game, Davis boarded a plane, flew overnight to Washington, took a taxi straight to the hospital, and arrived to find Lombardi alive, alert, but looking almost skeletal on his deathbed.

Lombardi smiled broadly and greeted the former Packer. "Willie," Coach said, "you're the best deal I ever made. I just want you to know that you were a great player."[126] Lombardi was so weak that Davis only stayed for two minutes—but Davis later said that those two minutes with Lombardi were worth the overnight trip. In fact, he was the last of Lombardi's players to see him alive.

Father Tim Moore, Lombardi's friend since St. Cecelia days, came to Washington to visit and comfort him. "I'm not afraid to die," Lombardi said. "But there's so much yet to be done in the world."[127]

In his short span of 57 years, Vince Lombardi had accomplished so much—yet it was clear that there is something he had hoped to accomplish in his life, something far greater than a string of NFL championships. What did he envision? What did he have in mind when he said, "There's so much yet to be done in the world"?

We don't know what Vince Lombardi hoped to achieve, had he lived two or three more decades. We just know that he had wanted to serve the human race and improve the lives of people around the world. Whatever Lombardi's vision for improving the world, it would have to remain undone. This was one fight Vince Lombardi would not win.

Vince Lombardi died at 7:12 a.m. on September 3, 1970, just 57 years old. He left a loving wife, both parents, two children, six grandchildren—and countless players and fans who loved him.

Lombardi's longtime secretary in Green Bay, Lori Keck, told me, "The day he passed away was terrible. I would always wake up with my clock radio set to Paul Harvey. I woke up that morning, and it was raining that day. And the first thing I heard from my radio was Paul Harvey saying, 'The heavens are weeping today over Green Bay because Vince Lombardi has died.'"

Her voice shook and she choked up. "It's been forty-five years," she added, "and I still can't talk about it without getting emotional. A very sad day. He died too soon."

Coach Lombardi's funeral and Robert F. Kennedy's were said to be the two largest services held at St. Patrick's Cathedral in New York. All along the route of the funeral cortege, the streets were lined with grieving fans.

After Vince Lombardi died, many of those who knew him best felt they had lost someone who was more than a mere coach. It was almost like losing a parent. Willie Davis summed up his own deep grief: "It was very much like how I felt when I lost my mother."[128]

When the death of a coach stirs such a depth of emotion and sorrow in his players, you know that he was much more than a coach. He was a friend, a mentor—

And a beloved servant.

LOMBARDI, THE COMPLETE LEADER

The quality of any man's life has got to be a full measure
of that man's personal commitment to excellence and
to victory, regardless of what field he may be in.
—**Vince Lombardi**

Vince Lombardi was a man of extremes, a bundle of contradictions.

He would scream and swear at his players, yet he also preached unconditional love, prayed daily, and attended church—not weekly, as most devout Christians do, but *every single day* without fail. At home, he would yell but not swear. His daughter Susan recalled that, almost immediately after losing his temper and yelling at her, he'd turn right around and apologize.

Lombardi spent most of his adult life coaching football, which he himself called "a violent game." Yet he also loved opera, especially Giacomo Puccini's *Madame Butterfly*, which he listened to many evenings at home, played on a reel-to-reel tape deck in his living room (he enjoyed playing it for visitors and family and would retell the tragic story along with the music). As for popular music, he liked the swing crooners—Frank Sinatra, Dean Martin, Tony Bennett—and was especially fond of Bobby Darin's rendition of "Mack the Knife."

Though Lombardi was to the game of football what General Patton was to the art of war, the tough-as-nails coach enjoyed some surprisingly homebody-ish pastimes. When he was feeling tense and anxious, often in the weeks before training camp, Marie would find Vince going through the house, cleaning out and tidying up all the closets. Lombardi was certainly not a chef—his culinary skills began and ended with grilled steaks and scrambled eggs. Yet, one of his favorite pastimes was sitting in an easy chair and reading cookbooks from cover to cover, as if they were novels. He preferred books on Italian cooking, but any kind of cookbook would do. He'd sometimes tell Marie about a particular dish he'd found that she should fix sometime, though she never did (she preferred to eat out).

Another of Lombardi's contradictions was the fact that this highly educated, relentlessly rational leader of men could be a bit superstitious at times. Royce Boyles told me a story about Lombardi's proclivity toward "lucky" talismans. Lombardi, Royce said, was fastidious about his appearance and apparel. He never went out in public without making sure his shoes were shined, his tie straight, and his creases sharp. But one Sunday, Lombardi arrived at the stadium and discovered to his chagrin that he had forgotten to put on his belt. It wouldn't do for him to be constantly hiking up his pants during the game, so he located some binding twine and threaded it through the belt loops, tied it in a knot, then went out and coached the game. The Packers won—so, what do you suppose Coach Lombardi had tied around his waist at the *next* Packers game? Binding twine, natch!

Vince Lombardi was the greatest football coach in history—and he was a lovable eccentric. I love the quirks and contradictions in his personality. They humanize the legend and take a bit of the air out of the myth—and that makes Lombardi someone we can emulate and identify with.

Yes, he turned the worst football team in the NFL into the best in just two seasons. Yes, he never had a losing season in his ten years as an NFL head coach. Yes, he coached the Green Bay Packers to five world championships and was inducted into the Hall of Fame in 1971. Yes, the Super Bowl trophy is named in his honor—and rightly so. But Vince Lombardi was not Superman. He was a man, with his share of interesting quirks and flaws—and that means we can learn lessons from his life, and we can apply those lessons to our own leadership lives every day.

Vince Lombardi was authentic. He was always himself in every setting. He was comfortable in his own skin. He didn't try to change who he was depending on the situation he was in or the people he was with. Lombardi was the real deal.

Though he learned from other coaches, he never tried to copy other coaches. He never tried to be anything he was not. Lombardi coached from within the zone of his own personality, his own strengths and weaknesses, his own self-awareness and self-confidence. Ultimately, everything about the Green Bay Packers—from the Packers Sweep to the tailoring of the green Packers sports coat—reflected the personality, the values, and the vision of Vince Lombardi. "In all my years of coaching," he once said, "I have never been successful using somebody else's plays."[129]

Coach Lombardi's story has a mythic quality to it, the makings of great drama. He was a working-class kid from Brooklyn who was obsessed with one thing—the game of football. He loved it, he dreamed about it, he made it his life. For 20 years, he toiled in obscurity, almost always an assistant, save for a head-coaching stint at a tiny Catholic high school. Just when he began to despair of ever being offered a head-coaching job, the worst team in the NFL came knocking. No, Lombardi was not the Packers' first choice, and they were not his, but Lombardi seized the opportunity —

And made football history.

He also gave us a leadership model worth studying and applying. Many people have tried to without success. Why? Because they didn't look closely enough. They didn't understand the real secret of his success.

One sports columnist wrote in the *Huffington Post*, "Vince Lombardi is arguably the worst thing that's ever happened to sports in America." This writer proceeded to blame Lombardi's "autocratic, kick 'em-in-the-butt coaching style" for producing a sports culture in which the head coach is required to be "a macho drill sergeant in order to be truly effective."[130] Well, anyone who thinks that's all there is to Vince Lombardi's leadership philosophy hasn't done his homework. He certainly hasn't described the *real* Vince Lombardi.

By examining the career of Coach Lombardi through the lens of the Seven Sides of Leadership, by studying everything that has been written about Lombardi, and by interviewing everyone still living who has ever known him or played for him, I have tried to delve beneath the surface of the legend to find the reality of Vince Lombardi. No one should be able to read all of the interviews in this book and conclude that Lombardi was just an "autocratic, kick 'em-in-the-butt" coach. Vince Lombardi didn't coach his teams to the top by bullying and screaming and swearing. He coached them to the top by being a complete seven-sided leader.

Coach Lombardi's players didn't play their hearts out for him out of fear. He had a magical, mystical influence over them because he made them better players, he made them believe in themselves, he made them reach deep down and discover skills and strengths and stamina and abilities they didn't even know they had. That's why Coach Lombardi's players won championships. That's why they played hard for him and won for him. That's why they respected him and loved him and why they wept for him when he died. If you don't understand that, then you don't understand Lombardi's greatness, and you don't understand leadership.

Yes, Vince Lombardi was a tough coach. But he succeeded because he made his players better. Not just better football players—better human beings.

That's why Vince Lombardi was a role model of leadership. By studying his example and understanding the lessons of his life, we can become better coaches, better executives, better teachers, better preachers, and better leaders in any arena of life. Coach Vince Lombardi exemplified all Seven Sides of Leadership:

1. *Vision.* He was able to envision a brighter future for his teams, and he charted a course for getting there. He didn't foresee the future—he made the future happen.

2. *Communication Skills.* He had the ability to communicate persuasively, to teach his concepts and principles effectively, to preach his values and philosophy convincingly, and to instill his fiery passion into their souls. Lombardi was an effective public speaker, and he used the power of his voice to motivate and inspire his players.

3. *People Skills.* He was a master psychologist who understood what made his players tick and how to get them to work in sync to achieve their common goals. He didn't treat them all the same—he treated them as individuals, and they respected and loved him for it.

4. *Character.* Coach Lombardi was not a perfect man, but he was a man of character and influence. His players bought into his agenda because they knew they could trust his character. Vince Lombardi was a man of leadership influence because he was a man of genuine character.

5. *Competence.* He let his players know from the get-go that he had the competence and competitiveness to lead them to victory. Great leaders inspire confidence through their competence and success—and that's why Coach Lombardi's players were inspired and motivated to play their hearts out for him.

6. *Boldness.* Vince Lombardi was bold, decisive, courageous, and confident. He made decisions and stuck to them. He never showed doubt or indecision. His confidence in himself enabled his players to believe in themselves. Confidence is contagious and leads to daring, decisive, successful action on the field.

7. *A Serving Heart.* This is the dimension of Vince Lombardi's leadership model that all too many people miss. I often wonder why he was so frequently misunderstood. It wasn't as if he hid his serving heart from view—he practically wore it on his sleeve! Lombardi was constantly talking about the serving dimension, the

need for love among the players, the need for humility and surrendering one's ego for the good of the team. Lombardi set the example for his players, and they followed his example—and became champions along the way.

Vince Lombardi had all seven of these qualities—the Seven Sides of Leadership. He was complete as a leader, and that completeness made him great. In fact, his completeness made him a legend.

Leadership is measured by results, and the leadership of Coach Vince Lombardi speaks for itself. Vision, communication skills, people skills, character, competence, boldness, and a serving heart—these seven principles are the keys to becoming a leader of excellence. Build these seven qualities into your own leadership life, and see how far they take you.

As Coach Lombardi himself would tell you, "To be successful in life demands that we make a personal commitment to excellence and to victory, even though the ultimate victory can never be completely won. Yet that victory might be pursued and wooed with every fiber of our body, with every bit of our might and all our effort. And each week, there is a new encounter; each day, there is a new challenge."[131]

I believe you have the makings of a legendary leader—that's why you've been reading this book. Now it's time to go and apply these lessons to your daily life.

Every Thursday morning before practice, Coach Lombardi would gather his players and give them a short motivational talk. Within minutes, he'd have them fired up. Their blood was pumping, and the hair was standing up on the back of their necks.

Then, before they went out the door to the practice field, Lombardi would issue this challenge: "Who's going to lead today?"

That's a good question for you and me to consider: Who is going to lead today? And who's going to lead tomorrow? Is it you?

Be a leader, my friend. And be a winner.

ABOUT THE AUTHORS

PAT WILLIAMS (ORLANDO, FLORIDA)

Pat Williams is the co-founder and senior vice president of the NBA's Orlando Magic. He is also a popular motivational speaker averaging over 150 appearances a year. Williams spent 50 years in professional baseball and basketball as a player and executive. He served as general manager of the 1983 world champion Philadelphia 76ers and managed both the Chicago Bulls and Atlanta Hawks.

Williams is the author of over 75 books. He and his wife, Ruth, are the parents of 19 children, including 14 adopted from four nations. He and his family have been featured on major network shows such as Good Morning America, The Today Show, Fox & Friends, and Mike and Mike as well as in such diverse publications as *Sports Illustrated, Reader's Digest, Good Housekeeping, The Wall Street Journal,* and *Focus on the Family.*

JIM DENNEY (CALIFORNIA)

Jim Denney has written more than 120 books, both fiction and nonfiction. He is the author of *Answers to Satisfy the Soul, Writing in Overdrive, Write Fearlessly!,* and the Timebenders science-fantasy series for young readers—*Battle Before Time, Doorway to Doom, Invasion of the Time Troopers,* and *Lost in Cydonia.*

CONTACT

You can contact Pat Williams at:
Pat Williams
c/o Orlando Magic
8701 Maitland Summit Boulevard
Orlando, FL 32810
phone: 407-916-2404
pwilliams@orlandomagic.com

Visit Pat Williams's Web site at:
www.PatWilliams.com

If you would like to set up a speaking engagement for Pat Williams, please call or write his assistant, Andrew Herdliska, at the above address, or call him at 407-916-2401. Requests can also be faxed to 407-916-2986 or e-mailed to **aherdliska@orlandomagic.com**.

We would love to hear from you. Please send your comments about this book to Pat Williams at the above address. Thank you.

NOTES

[1] Harry Laver and Jeffrey J. Matthews (Eds), *The Art of Command: Military Leadership from George Washington to Colin Powell* (Lexington, KY: The University Press of Kentucky, 2008), x.

[2] Aubrey Malphurs, *Developing a Vision for Ministry in the 21st Century* (Grand Rapids: Baker, 1999), 75–76.

[3] Ed Gruver, *The Ice Bowl: The Cold Truth About Football's Most Unforgettable Game* (Ithaca, NY: McBooks Press, 1998), 36.

[4] Michael O'Brien, *Vince: A Personal Biography of Vince Lombardi* (New York: HarperCollins, 1987), 46.

[5] Chris Havel, *Lombardi—An Illustrated Life* (Iola, WI: Krause Publications, 011), 19.

[6] David Maraniss, *When Pride Still Mattered: A Life of Vince Lombardi* (New York: Simon & Schuster, 1999), 145–146.

[7] Donald T. Phillips, *Run to Win: Vince Lombardi on Coaching and Leadership* (New York: St. Martin's, 2007), 118.

[8] David Maraniss, *When Pride Still Mattered*, 160.

[9] David Maraniss, *When Pride Still Mattered*, 165.

[10] Jonathan Rand, *The Year That Changed the Game: The Memorable Months That Shaped Pro Football* (Washington, DC: Potomac Books, 2008), 27.

[11] Joe Ehrmann, *InSideOut Coaching: How Sports Can Transform Lives* (New York: Simon & Schuster, 2011), 76.

[12] David Maraniss, 193.

[13] David Maraniss, *When Pride Still Mattered*, 199.

[14] Chuck Johnson, "Packers Hire Vince Lombardi," *Milwaukee Journal Sentinel*, January 29, 1959, www.jsonline.com/sports/packers/164346156.html.

[15] David Maraniss, *When Pride Still Mattered*, 202.

[16] David Claerbaut, *Bart Starr: When Leadership Mattered* (Lanham, MD: Taylor, 2004), 112.

[17] Donald T. Phillips, 14–15.

[18] Bud Lea, "Plain and Simple: Ray Nitschke Was the Packers," *Milwaukee Journal Sentinel*, April 1, 1998, www.jsonline.com/sports/packers/215012441.html.

[19] Donald T. Phillips, 104.

[20] Gene Wojciechowski, "Lombardi Turned Packers into Winners," ESPN.com, February 3, 2006, http://sports.espn.go.com/espn/columns/story?id=2318158.

[21] Lieutenant Colonel Belinda L. Buckman, United States Army, "Vince Lombardi As a Strategic Leader," U.S. Army War College, Carlisle Barracks, Pennsylvania, February 22, 2002, 10–11, handle.dtic.mil/100.2/ADA400769.

[22] Lieutenant Colonel Buckman, 11.

[23] Keith Dunnavant, *America's Quarterback: Bart Starr and the Rise of the National Football League* (New York: St. Martin's, 2011), 126.

[24] LuckyLaRue17, "Vince Lombardi Teaches the Power Sweep 1," YouTube.com, October 17, 2010, www.youtube.com/watch?v=kmtVeqMt6dc, transcribed by the authors.

[25] David Maraniss, *When Pride Still Mattered*, 446.

[26] Jeff Olson, *The Light Edge: Turning Simple Disciplines into Massive Success & Happiness* (Austin, TX: Greenleaf, 2005), 253.

[27] 1 Corinthians 9:24, paraphrased.

[28] Dan Lauria, "Vince Lombardi of Broadway: Dan Lauria Reflects on NFL Icon," NFL.com, June 11, 2013, www.nfl.com/news/story/0ap1000000210631/article/vince-lombardi-of-broadway-dan-lauria-reflects-on-nfl-icon.

[29] Patrick McCaskey, *Pillars of the NFL: Coaches Who Have Won Three or More Championships* (Crystal Lake, IL: Sporting Chance Press, 2014), 199.

[30] Vince Lombardi, Jr., *The Lombardi Rules: 26 Lessons from Vince Lombardi, the World's Greatest Coach* (New York: McGraw-Hill, 2002), 53–54.

[31] Vince Lombardi, "Famous Quotes by Vince Lombardi," VinceLombardi.com, 2010, www.vincelombardi.com/quotes.html.

[32] Ibid.

[33] W. C. Heinz, edited by Bill Littlefield, *The Top of His Game: The Best Sportswriting of W. C. Heinz* (New York: Library of America, 2015), 448.

[34] Jackson Michael, *The Game Before the Money: Voices of the Men Who Built the NFL* (Lincoln, NE: University of Nebraska Press, 2014), 101–102.

[35] Jerry Kramer, "Winning Wasn't Everything," *New York Times*, January 24, 1997, www.nytimes.com/ref/opinion/06opclassic.html?_r=0.

[36] Matthew 26:41, *Holy Bible, New International Version®*, NIV® Copyright ©1973, 1978, 1984, 2011 by Biblica, Inc.® Used by permission. All rights reserved worldwide.

[37] John Schulian, *Football: Great Writing About the National Sport* (New York: Library of America, 2014), 219.

[38] Bob Oates, *Football in America: Game of the Century* (Coal Valley, IL: Quality Sports Publications, 1999), 232.

[39] Vince Lombardi with W. C. Heinz, *Run to Daylight!: Vince Lombardi's Diary of One Week with the Green Bay Packers* (New York: Simon & Schuster, 1963/2014), 15–16.

[40] Brian Cronin, "Sports Legend Revealed: Did Vince Lombardi Trade a Player Five Minutes After Learning the Player Hired an Agent?," Los Angeles Times Blogs, February 8, 2011, http://latimesblogs.latimes.com/sports_blog/2011/02/sports-legend-revealed-did-vince-lombardi-trade-a-player-five-minutes-after-learning-the-player-hire.html.

[41] Jackson Michael, *The Game Before the Money*, 132.

[42] Bob Starkey, "The Other Side of Vince Lombardi," Hoops Thoughts, October 2, 2009, http://hoopthoughts.blogspot.com/2009/10/other-side-of-vince-lombardi.html.

[43] Donald T. Phillips, Run to Win, 58–60.

[44] Edward Gruver, *Nitschke* (Lanham, MD: Rowman & Littlefield, 2002), xi.

[45] Gruver, *Nitschke*, xi.

[46] Gruver, *Nitschke*, 63–64.

[47] Gruver, *Nitschke*, xii.

[48] Gruver, *Nitschke*, 64.

[49] Bud Lea, "Plain and Simple: Ray Nitschke Was the Packers."

[50] Rich Eisen, *Total Access: A Journey to the Center of the NFL Universe* (New York: St. Martin's, 2007), 248.

[51] Malcolm Gladwell, "True Grit," *The New York Review of Books*, February 24, 2000, www.nybooks.com/articles/archives/2000/feb/24/true-grit/.

[52] David Maraniss, *When Pride Still Mattered*, 243–244.

[53] David Maraniss, "Coach, Symbol, Savior," ESPN, March 5, 2002, http://espn.go.com/page2/wash/s/2002/0305/1346027.html.

[54] David Maraniss, *When Pride Still Mattered*, 245.

[55] Ian O'Connor, "Gospel of St. Vince," ESPN.go.com, January 23, 2014, http://espn.go.com/espn/feature/story/_/id/10304484/gospel-st-vince.

[56] Malcolm Gladwell, "True Grit."

[57] Ibid.

[58] Ibid.

[59] Donald T. Phillips, *Run to Win*, 24.

[60] Jerry Kramer, "A Century of Vince Lombardi," NFL AM, NFL Network, June 11, 2013, www.packers.com/media-center/videos/Jerry-Kramer-shares-Vince-Lombardi-stories/4acc87b3-54fb-45ac-b993-b40e35a6aa47.

[61] Chuck Carlson, *Game of My Life: 25 Stories of Packers Football* (Champaign, IL: Sports Publishing, LLC, 2004), p. 149.

[62] Donald T. Phillips, *Run to Win*, 24.

[63] Vince Lombardi Jr., *What It Takes to Be #1: Vince Lombardi on Leadership* (New York: McGraw-Hill, 2003), 255.

[64] Thom Loverro, *Hail Victory: An Oral History of the Washington Redskins* (Hoboken, NJ: John Wiley & Sons, 2006), 78.

[65] Vince Lombardi Jr., *What It Takes to Be #1*, 116.

[66] Vince Lombardi Jr., *What It Takes to Be #1*, 204–205.

[67] Michael Sheard, *Mental Toughness: The Mindset Behind Sporting Achievement*, Second Edition (New York: Routledge, 2010), 28.

[68] Ed Gruver, *The Ice Bowl: The Cold Truth about Football's Most Unforgettable Game* (Ithaca, NY: McBooks Press, 1998), 36.

[69] Ian O'Connor, "Gospel of St. Vince," ESPN.go.com, January 23, 2014, http://espn.go.com/espn/feature/story/_/id/10304484/gospel-st-vince.

[70] Ed Gruver, *The Ice Bowl*, 34.

[71] Ibid.

[72] Ed Gruver, *The Ice Bowl*, 35.

[73] David Maraniss, *When Pride Still Mattered*, 240.

[74] Ibid.

[75] Jerry Kramer, "Winning Wasn't Everything."

[76] Willie Davis with Jim Martyka and Andrea Erickson Davis, *Closing the Gap: Lombardi, the Packers Dynasty, and the Pursuit of Excellence* (Chicago: Triumph Books, 2012), vii.

[77] Jeré Longman, "Eagles' 1960 Victory Was an N.F.L. Turning Point," *New York Times*, January 6, 2011, www.nytimes.com/2011/01/07/sports/football/07eagles.html.

[78] Warren G. Bennis, *The Essential Bennis: Essays on Leadership* (San Francisco: Jossey-Bass, 2009), 229, 230.

[79] John C. Maxwell, *The 21 Indispensable Qualities of a Leader: Becoming the Person Others Will Want to Follow* (Nashville: Thomas Nelson, 1999), 30.

[80] Jerry Izenberg, *Rozelle: A Biography* (Lincoln, NE: University of Nebraska Press, 2014), 151.

81 Vince Lombardi, "Famous Quotes by Vince Lombardi," VinceLombardi.com, www.vincelombardi.com/quotes.html.

82 James A. Michener, *Sports in America* (New York: Ballantine, 1983), 520.

83 Vince Lombardi with W. C. Heinz, *Run to Daylight!: Vince Lombardi's Diary of One Week with the Green Bay Packers* (New York: Simon & Schuster, 1963/2014), 192.

84 Vince Lombardi Jr., *What It Takes to Be #1*, 234.

85 Vince Lombardi, "What It Takes to Be Number One," VinceLombardi.com, 2010, www.vincelombardi.com/number-one.html.

86 David Claerbaut, *Bart Starr: When Leadership Mattered* (Lanham, MD: Rowman & Littlefield, 2004), 224.

87 Donald T. Phillips, *Run to Win*, 171.

88 Byron Williams, "A Misreading of Lombardi," Huffington Post, The Blog, January 19, 2015, www.huffingtonpost.com/byron-williams/a-misreading-of-lombardi_b_6185110.html.

89 Peter A. French, *Ethics and College Sports: Ethics, Sports, and the University* (Lanham, MD: Rowman & Littlefield, 2004), 35.

90 Donald T. Phillips, *Run to Win*, 20.

91 Donald T. Phillips, *Run to Win*, 22.

92 Jason Selk, *Executive Toughness: the Mental Training Program to Increase Your Leadership Performance* (New York: McGraw-Hill, 2012), 126.

93 R. Cort Kirkwood, *Real Men: Ten Courageous Americans to Know and Admire* (Nashville: Cumberland House, 2006), 62.

94 Willie Davis with Jim Martyka and Andrea Erickson Davis, *Closing the Gap*, 67.

95 Ian O'Connor, "Gospel of St. Vince."; David Maraniss, *When Pride Still Mattered*, 72–73.

96 Author uncredited, "Monolithic Packers–Bears Rivalry Evokes Numerous Memories," Packers.com, September 16, 2004, www0.nfl.packers.com/news/stories/2004/09/16/2/printable/?i=2004/09/16/2/.

97 Cliff Christl, "Lombardi Regretted Fourth-and-One Calls," Packers.com, April 23, 2015, www.packers.com/news-and-events/article-cliffs-notes/article-1/Lombardi-regretted-fourth-and-1-calls/6a2451d0-ca13-43bb-993f-26bd4de26e3b.

98 Author uncredited, "Suspensions of Hornung, Karras Rocked NFL," *Washington Times*, April 16, 2007, www.washingtontimes.com/news/2007/apr/16/20070416-122710-4602r/?page=all.

99 Vince Lombardi Jr., *What It Takes to Be #1*, 30.

100 ChatSports Staff, "Five Infamous Games That Every NFL Fan Should Know by

Name," ChatSports.com, July 17, 2014, www.chatsports.com/nfl/a/5-Infamous-Games-That-Every-NFL-Fan-Should-Know-By-Name-10-206-1810.

[101] Keith Whitmire, "Tom Landry: In His Own Words," *Chicago Tribune* (reprinted from the *Dallas Morning News*), February 20, 2000, http://articles.chicagotribune.com/2000-02-20/sports/0002200005_1_big-decision-ice-bowl-don-meredith.

[102] Jackson Michael, *The Game Before the Money*, 84.

[103] This quote by an NFL official was related to me by longtime pro football executive Ernie Accorsi.

[104] Vince Lombardi Jr., *What It Takes to Be #1*, 100.

[105] Ian O'Connor, "Gospel of St. Vince."

[106] Allen St. John, "Coach," *New York Times*, October 10, 1999, www.nytimes.com/books/99/10/10/reviews/991010.10stjoht.html.

[107] David Maraniss, "Coach, Symbol, Savior."

[108] Jack Moore, "Vince Lombardi Isn't Who You Think He Is," Vice Sports, October 30, 2014, https://sports.vice.com/en_us/article/vince-lombardi-isnt-who-you-think-he-is.

[109] Lee Iacocca with William Novak, *Iacocca: An Autobiography* (New York: Bantam, 1984), 60.

[110] Donald T. Phillips, *Run to Win*, 23.

[111] Vince Lombardi Jr., *What It Takes to Be #1*, 91.

[112] Bart Starr with Murray Olderman, *Starr: My Life in Football* (New York: Morrow, 1987), 88.

[113] David Maraniss, *When Pride Still Mattered*, 248.

[114] Donald T. Phillips, *Run to Win*, 171.

[115] "Mr. Lambeau" (pen name of blogger), "Sports Illustrated: March 3, 1969," Packerville U.S.A., February 22, 2007, http://packerville.blogspot.com/2007/02/sports-illustrated-march-3-1969.html.

[116] Associated Press, "Lombardi Retires As Packer Coach, but Keeps GM Job," *Sarasota Herald-Tribune*, February 2, 1968, 33.

[117] Patsy Neal, *Sport and Identity* (Philadelphia: Dorrance & Co., 1972), 23.

[118] Dave Brady, "'I Will Demand a Commitment To Excellence,' New Chief Says," *Washington Post*, February 7, 1969, www.washingtonpost.com/wp-srv/sports/redskins/longterm/1997/history/allart/vince_hired.htm.

[119] Dave Klein, *The Vince Lombardi Story* (New York: Lion Books, 1971), 123–124.

[120] David Maraniss, "Coach, Symbol, Savior."

[121] Jackson Michael, *The Game Before the Money*, 100.

[122] Brooke Kroeger, *Passing: When People Can't Be Who They Are* (New York: Public Affairs, 2003), 238.

[123] Jim Corbett, "Vince Lombardi Might Have Been Perfect Coach for Michael Sam," *USA Today*, February 11, 2014, www.usatoday.com/story/sports/nfl/draft/2014/02/11/vince-lombardi-michael-sam-gay-acceptance/5395467/.

[124] Ian O'Connor, "Lombardi: A Champion of Gay Rights," ESPN.com, May 4, 2013, http://espn.go.com/new-york/nfl/story/_/id/9237535/vince-lombardi-proud-jason-collins.

[125] David Maraniss, "Coach, Symbol, Savior."

[126] Chris Havel, *Lombardi—An Illustrated Life* (Iola, WI: Krause Publications, 2011), 62.

[127] David Maraniss, *When Pride Still Matterred*, 497.

[128] Chris Havel, *Lombardi—An Illustrated Life*, 62.

[129] Vince Lombardi Jr., *What It Takes to Be #1*, 56.

[130] Ken Reed, "It's Time to Bench Tyrannical Coaches," *Huffington Post*, November 1, 2013, www.huffingtonpost.com/ken-reed/sports-coaches_b_4195220.html.

[131] Adapted from a quote by Vince Lombardi, "Famous Quotes by Vince Lombardi," VinceLombardi.com, 2010, www.vincelombardi.com/quotes.html. Lombardi's original words were: "Most important of all, to be successful in life demands that a man make a personal commitment to excellence and to victory, even though the ultimate victory can never be completely won. Yet that victory might be pursued and wooed with every fiber of our body, with every bit of our might and all our effort. And each week, there is a new encounter; each day, there is a new challenge."

www.ingramcontent.com/pod-product-compliance
Lightning Source LLC
Jackson TN
JSHW011948131224
75386JS00042B/1609